World Wonders 1

GRAMMAR

Alexandra Green

T0349574

NATIONAL GEOGRAPHIC LEARNING | CENGAGE Learning

Australia • Brazil • Japan • Korea • Mexico • Singapore • Spain • United Kingdom • United States

World Wonders 1 Grammar
Student's Book

Alexandra Green

Publisher: Jason Mann

Director of Content Development: Sarah Bideleux

Assistant Development Editor: Kaye Lafyati

Art Director/Cover designer: Natasa Arsenidou

Graphic design/Composition: Tania Diakaki

National Geographic Editorial Liaison:
Leila Hishmeh

Acknowledgements

Illustrated by Panagiotis Angeletakis,
Alexia Lougiaki

For permission to use material from this text or product, submit all requests online at **cengage.com/permissions**

Further permissions questions can be emailed to **permissionrequest@cengage.com**

ISBN: 978-1-4240-5842-6

National Geographic Learning
Cheriton House, North Way, Andover, Hampshire,
SP10 5BE United Kingdom

Cengage Learning is a leading provider of customised learning solutions with office locations around the globe, including Singapore, the United Kingdom, Australia, Mexico, Brazil and Japan.

Cengage Learning products are represented in Canada by Nelson Education Ltd.

Visit National Geographic Learning online at **ngl.cengage.com**
Visit our corporate website at **www.cengage.com**

Photo credits

We are grateful to the following for permission to reproduce copyright photographs: Brian J. Skerry/National Geographic Image Collection, Ed George/National Geographic Image Collection, George Grall/National Geographic Image Collection, Alaska Stock Images/National Geographic Image Collection, Kenneth Garrett/National Geographic Image Collection, Colin Monteath/Minden Pictures/National Geographic Image Collection

Printed in the United Kingdom by Ashford Colour Press Ltd
Print Number: 09   Print Year: 2020

Contents

Introduction to World Wonders Grammar

Welcome to *World Wonders Grammar*, a four-level grammar course that has been designed to cover the needs of students at beginner to intermediate levels. *World Wonders 1 Grammar* accompanies *World Wonders 1 Student's Book*, but it can also be used with any other beginner course.

World Wonders 1 Grammar Student's Book

The student's book consists of an introduction, twelve units and six reviews. Each unit contains two or three lessons. The wide variety of task types, including picture-based and photo-based tasks, will keep students motivated and help them to grasp the grammar points easily. The book is of a manageable length and can be completed in one school year. The amount of time spent on individual grammar points will largely depend on teaching situations and the ability of the students.

Each lesson begins with a cartoon presentation designed to introduce the grammar in an amusing way. This is followed by grammar theory with example sentences. *Remember!* boxes appear often and serve to remind students of things they should be aware of. The lesson then continues with a selection of graded grammar tasks before finishing with the speaking task. The speaking tasks have been carefully written to encourage students to practise the grammar points they have just learnt in realistic situations.

There is a review after every two units of *World Wonders 1 Grammar*. Each review contains a variety of tasks designed to consolidate the grammar covered in the preceding two units. The review ends with a non-fiction Writing Project featuring National Geographic photography. Students then have the opportunity to do their own Writing Project.

At the back of the book there is an alphabetical word list of key vocabulary for each lesson.

World Wonders 1 Grammar Teacher's Book

The key to the student's book tasks is overprinted for easy reference. There are six photocopiable tests at the back of the teacher's book; one for every two units of *World Wonders 1 Grammar*. The key to the tests is also included.

A / An, Plurals, Demonstratives, Subject Pronouns & Prepositions of Time

A / An

We use **a** and **an** (the indefinite articles) with singular nouns.
a snake
an orange

We use **a** before nouns that begin with a consonant (b, c, d, f, g, h, i, j, k, l, m, n, p, q, r, s, t, v, w, x, y, z).
a boat
a tree

We use **an** before nouns that begin with a vowel (a, e, i, o, u).
an elephant
an island

Sometimes there is an adjective before the noun. We use **a** when the adjective begins with a consonant.

We use **an** when the adjective begins with a vowel.
a new album
an amazing game

We use **a** or **an** to talk about one person, animal or thing in general.
There is a spider in the kitchen.
He's got a new bag.

Remember!

 Be careful with words that begin with h or u! When the word begins with a consonant sound, we use a. When the word begins with a vowel sound, we use an.
a house, an hour, a uniform, an uncle

1 **Write a or an.**

1	_an_ eye	4	_____ door	7	_____ egg
2	_____ green apple	5	_____ ear	8	_____ exciting hobby
3	_____ box	6	_____ hour	9	_____ hospital

Plurals

We usually add **–s** to a noun to make it plural.
pen   pens
hut   huts
book   books

We add **–es** to nouns that end in **–s**, **–ss**, **–sh**, **–ch** and **–x**.
box   boxes
beach   beaches
watch   watches

When a word ends in a consonant + **–y**, we take off the **-y** and add **-ies**.
family   families
lady   ladies
party   parties

When a word ends in a vowel + **–y**, we just add **-s**.
day   days
boy   boys
toy   toys

We usually add **–s** to nouns that end in **–o**, but we sometimes add **–es**.
photo   photos
tomato   tomatoes
potato   potatoes

When a noun ends in **–f**, or **–fe**, we usually take off the **–f** or **–fe** and add **–ves**. We just add **-s** to the words **giraffe** and **roof**.
wife   wives
knife   knives
life   lives
giraffe   giraffes
roof   roofs

Remember!

 Some nouns are irregular and they do not follow these rules.

child	children	mouse	mice
fish	fish	sheep	sheep
foot	feet	tooth	teeth
man	men	woman	women

2 **Write the plural of these words.**

box   child   leaf   mouse   pencil   photo   toy   watch

1 four _____watches_____

2 fifteen _____

3 four _____

4 two _____

5 nine _____

6 eight _____

7 three _____

8 five _____

Demonstratives

We use demonstratives to show that someone or something is near us (**this, these**) or further away (**that, those**).

Singular	Plural
this	these
that	those

---

3 **Complete the sentences with This, That, These or Those.**

1 _____These_____ are my shoes.

2 _____ is my phone.

3 _____ bird is beautiful.

4 _____ is your ruler.

5 _____ flowers are very nice.

6 _____ are my chocolates!

6

Subject Pronouns

Subject pronouns show who or what something is or does.
I am Sally.
She plays tennis.

We use **it** for animals and things. When the animal is our pet, we often use **he** or **she**.
It's a funny pet.
This is Sooty. He's my cat.

We use **you** for both singular and plural.
You are very tall.
You are my friends.

We use **they** for two or more people, animals or things.
They are nice people.

Singular	Plural
I	we
you	you
he	they
she	
it	

4 **Complete the sentences with subject pronouns.**

1 _____She_____ is my friend. (Sally)
2 _____ are at school. (Pat and Freddie)
3 _____ isn't in the kitchen. (Lucinda)
4 _____ haven't got a black dog. (you and Alistair)
5 _____ is very small. (the bird)
6 _____ are on the table. (the eggs)
7 _____ is tall. (Matthew)
8 _____ are fine, thank you. (Clare and I)

Prepositions of Time

at	in	on
at six o'clock	in the morning/afternoon/evening	on Monday/Wednesday
at night	in 1998/2009	on Thursday evening
at the weekend	in winter/spring/summer/autumn	on 21st April
at Christmas/Easter	in May/September/December	on Christmas Day

5 **Complete the sentences with prepositions of time.**

1 It's warm _____in_____ summer.
2 My birthday is _____ 23rd September.
3 It's 10 o'clock _____ night!
4 We play games _____ Christmas Day.
5 Dinner is _____ 7 o'clock.
6 My aunt always comes to our house _____ my birthday.
7 We play tennis _____ Wednesdays.
8 I go to school _____ the morning.

Present Simple: Be

Me Polly, you John?

Yes, you are Polly and I am John. Nice to meet you, Polly!

Be

We use **be** with subject pronouns (I, you, he, etc) or with other nouns.
He is hungry.
Sharks are grey.

We use **be** to talk about someone's job, nationality, relationship or his or her name.
He is a scientist.
They are English.
We are sisters.
I am Jake.

We also use **be** to describe people or things.
Robbie is young.
The hut is old.

We use the short form in everyday English.
Hi, I'm Oliver.

Remember!

In English, there is no difference between you singular and you plural.

Affirmative	Negative	Question	Short answers	
I'm (I am)	I'm not (I am not)	Am I …?	Yes, I am.	No, I'm not.
you're (you are)	you aren't (you are not)	Are you …?	Yes, you are.	No, you aren't.
he's (he is)	he isn't (he is not)	Is he …?	Yes, he is.	No, he isn't.
she's (she is)	she isn't (she is not)	Is she …?	Yes, she is.	No, she isn't.
it's (it is)	it isn't (it is not)	Is it …?	Yes, it is.	No, it isn't.
we're (we are)	we aren't (we are not)	Are we …?	Yes, we are.	No, we aren't.
you're (you are)	you aren't (you are not)	Are you …?	Yes, you are.	No, you aren't.
they're (they are)	they aren't (they are not)	Are they …?	Yes, they are.	No, they aren't.

1 Write the sentences again with the short form of be.

1 You are very tall.   _You're very tall._

2 He is clever.   _____

3 We are not on holiday.   _____

4 I am in the garden.   _____

5 They are not cousins.   _____

6 She is not happy.   _____

7 They are funny tricks.   _____

8 It is not a good idea.   _____

2 Look at the picture and complete the sentences with the correct form of be.

1 The sea ____'s____ blue.

2 It _____ a beautiful day.

3 It _____ cold.

4 We _____ at the beach.

5 I _____ in the sea.

6 Ben and Harry _____ in the sea.

7 We _____ happy.

8 Holidays _____ cool!

3 Complete the sentences about you with the correct form of be.

1 I ____'m____ from Greece.

2 I _____ crazy about science.

3 My dad _____ a scientist.

4 My mum _____ beautiful.

5 My friends and I _____ at school now.

6 My cousins _____ funny.

7 I _____ nine years old.

8 My house _____ new.

4 Look at the picture and answer the questions.

1 Is the sky grey? _No, it isn't._   5 Is the dog big? _____
2 Are the girls happy? _____ 6 Is the door black? _____
3 Is the house small? _____   7 Is the boy tall? _____
4 Are the cats white? _____   8 Is the car old? _____

5 Complete the questions with **Am**, **Are** or **Is**. Then complete the short answers.

1 ___Is___ Kate your new friend?   5 _____ Misty and Molly big chimps?
   Yes, ___she is___ .   Yes, _____ .
2 _____ we crazy about school?   6 _____ I beautiful?
   No, _____ .   Yes, _____ .
3 _____ the sharks in the sea?   7 _____ you and Tom cousins?
   Yes, _____ .   No, _____ .
4 _____ David young?   8 _____ you twelve years old?
   No, _____ .   No, _____ .

6 Circle the correct words.

1 Is / Are we at the beach?
2 My cousin is / are cool.
3 Sharks isn't / aren't red.
4 Is / Are they sisters?
5 Uncle Joe isn't / aren't in the house.
6 I am / are in the water.
7 You isn't / aren't short.
8 Is / Are the baby happy?

Speaking

Ask and answer the questions with your partner.

Are you at the beach now?

No, I'm not.

- Is your school new?
- Is your best friend tall?
- Is your uncle a teacher?
- Is your classroom big?
- Are your cousins clever?
- Is your birthday in April?
- Are you twelve years old?

Possessive Adjectives

Possessive Adjectives

Possessive adjectives show that something belongs to someone or something. They go before the noun.
Mum is beautiful. Her hair is fair.
The hut is small. Its door is green.

Subject Pronouns	Possessive Adjectives
I	my
you	your
he	his
she	her
it	its
we	our
you	your
they	their

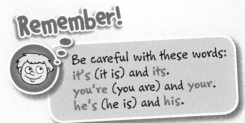

Remember!

Be careful with these words:
it's (it is) and its.
you're (you are) and your.
he's (he is) and his.

1 **Complete the sentences with possessive adjectives.**

1 This house is amazing! Is it ___your___ house? (you)

2 Amy is _____ sister. (I)

3 Elisabeth and I are cousins. _____ mothers are sisters. (we)

4 Is Mr Kelly _____ teacher? (she)

5 It's very warm in _____ house. (we)

6 Dad is 38 years old. _____ name is Mark. (he)

7 Is _____ father a scientist? (they)

8 The cat is white. _____ eyes are green. (it)

2 Look at the pictures and complete the sentences with these possessive adjectives.

her	its	~~my~~	our	their	your

1 This is me. I'm with ___my___ grandma.

2 Dad and I are with _____ dog, Moose.

3 Here's Mum. It's _____ birthday.

4 Look at you! _____ hair is very short!

5 Look at my fish. _____ names are Sharky and Nemo.

6 Here's my rabbit. _____ ears are big!

3 Match.

1 The girls are sisters.
2 I'm on holiday with Mum and Dad.
3 Grandma is very beautiful.
4 Nick is my best friend.
5 I'm at school.

a His birthday is in August.
b My classroom is small.
c Her eyes are dark green.
d Our hotel is on the beach.
e Their names are Cindy and Sally.

4 Circle the correct words.

1 The girls are happy. Its / Their dolls are beautiful.
2 This is my pet rabbit. Their / Its ears are very long.
3 Mr Shaw is next to his / its car.
4 Father penguins keep its / their eggs warm.
5 Lucy is crazy about her / its dog.
6 Josh and I are brothers. Our / Their eyes are brown.
7 I'm eleven years old today! It's her / my birthday.
8 You're clever. Its / Your idea is cool!

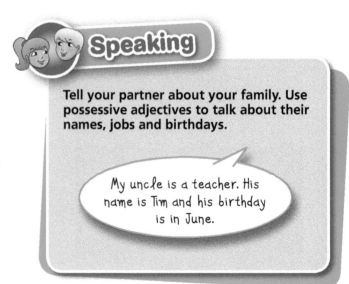

Speaking

Tell your partner about your family. Use possessive adjectives to talk about their names, jobs and birthdays.

My uncle is a teacher. His name is Tim and his birthday is in June.

Possessive 's

I'm hungry. A banana, cool!

Oh! It's the chimp's banana.

Oh no! It's the chimps' banana!

Possessive 's

We use **'s** to show that something belongs to someone or something.
This is Natalie's book.

We add **'s** to singular nouns.
This is the penguin's egg.

When the noun is plural, we add an apostrophe after the **-s**.
This is the boys' house.

But when the noun has an irregular plural, we add **'s**.
The children's hair is dark.
The women's daughters are beautiful.

---

1 **Complete the sentences with the possessive 's ('s or '). Use the words in brackets.**

1 The _____girl's_____ idea is great! (girl)

2 _____ lemonade is on the table. (Grandma)

3 The _____ dog is cool. (twins)

4 Your _____ cat is hungry. (friends)

5 My _____ job is amazing. (uncle)

6 The _____ grandad is in the water. (children)

7 Is the _____ mum in the hut? (boys)

8 The _____ sister is beautiful. (babies)

2 Look at the pictures and circle the correct words.

1 Jack is the girl's / girls' father.

2 The boy's / boys' hands are cold.

3 The chimp's / chimps' arms are long.

4 The penguin's / penguins' chick is beautiful.

5 The men's / man's wives aren't tall.

6 The bird's / birds' feet are red.

3 Choose the correct answers.

1 Is that your _____ brother?
   a fathers'   (b) father's

2 My _____ house is near the sea.
   a parent's   b parents'

3 _____ cousins are in Africa.
   a Mum's   b Mums'

4 The two _____ husbands are friends.
   a women's   b woman's

5 _____ friend is cool.
   a Dad's   b Dads'

6 What's the _____ name?
   a scientist's   b scientists'

7 My _____ names are Corrine, Bea and Sally.
   a sister's   b sisters'

8 The _____ birthday is in April.
   a man's   b men's

Speaking

Ask and answer questions with your partner about you, your family, your friends and your teachers.

What's your ....'s name?

Her/His name is ... .

• Is your ....'s house big?
• When is your ....'s birthday?
• What's your ....'s favourite colour?
• What's your ....'s favourite lesson?
• What's your ....'s favourite game?
• What's your dog's name?
• What's your cat's name?

Have got

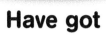

> Jenny, you've got lots of messages on your computer.

Have got

We use **have got** to describe someone or something.
The spider has got eight legs.

We use **have got** to show that something belongs to someone or something.
He's got a laptop.

Affirmative	Negative
I've got (I have got)	I haven't got (I have not got)
you've got (you have got)	you haven't got (you have not got)
he's got (he has got)	he hasn't got (he has not got)
she's got (she has got)	she hasn't got (she has not got)
it's got (it has got)	it hasn't got (it has not got)
we've got (we have got)	we haven't got (we have not got)
you've got (you have got)	you haven't got (you have not got)
they've got (they have got)	they haven't got (they have not got)

Question	Short answers	
Have I got ...?	Yes, I have.	No, I haven't.
Have you got ...?	Yes, you have.	No, you haven't.
Has he got ...?	Yes, he has.	No, he hasn't.
Has she got ...?	Yes, she has.	No, she hasn't.
Has it got ...?	Yes, it has.	No, it hasn't.
Have we got ...?	Yes, we have.	No, we haven't.
Have you got ...?	Yes, you have.	No, you haven't.
Have they got ...?	Yes, they have.	No, they haven't.

Remember!

Be careful with *its* (possessive adjective) and *it's* (it has) got.

15

1 Complete the sentences with the short form of **have got.**

1 She ___'s got___ a board game.

2 I _____ a new skateboard. It's cool!

3 You _____ a strange message. It's a mystery!

4 They _____ a real lizard.

5 We _____ lots of computer games.

6 The dog is happy. It _____ a ball.

2 Complete the sentences with the negative form of **have got.**

1 Mum and I ___haven't got___ a map with us.

2 I _____ a present for Dan.

3 My cousin Toby _____ a real robot.

4 The city _____ lots of museums.

5 You _____ a new toy.

6 Aunt Lila and Uncle Max _____ mobile phones.

3 Complete the questions using **have got** and the words in brackets. Then complete the short answers.

1 ___Have Liz and Pete got___ a magic pen? (Liz and Pete)

No, ___they haven't___ .

2 _____ a laptop? (you)

No, _____ .

3 _____ a house in Spain? (she)

Yes, _____ .

4 _____ a fast bike? (Jason)

Yes, _____ .

5 _____ the pieces of the puzzle? (we)

No, _____ .

6 _____ a pet? (I)

Yes, _____ .

4 Circle the correct words.

1 Josh haven't / (hasn't) got a picture of a dragon in his room.

2 Have / Has they got a new puzzle?

3 Sammy have / has got a house near the sea.

4 Have / Has you got a message on your mobile phone?

5 The children have / has got a teddy bear.

6 Have / Has Uncle Harry got a camera?

7 We haven't / hasn't got any boots.

8 Have / Has I got a spider in my hair?

16

5 Look at the pictures about Tom and Cindy and answer the questions.

1 Has Tom got a skateboard?

Yes, he has.

2 Have Tom and Cindy got bikes?

_____

3 Has Tom's father got a laptop?

_____

4 Has Cindy got lots of DVDs?

_____

5 Has Cindy's mum got a mobile phone?

_____

6 Has Tom got lots of homework?

_____

6 Put the words in the correct order to make sentences or questions.

1 big / got / have / dog / we / a   We have got a big dog. _____

2 ? / got / Aunt May / has / a / camera   _____

3 kite / got / cousins / my / a / haven't   _____

4 teacher / a / pen / got / our / has / magic   _____

5 ? / an / DVD / got / has / Nick / exciting   _____

6 ? / got / we / have / work / lots of / today   _____

 **Speaking**

Ask and answer questions with your partner about what you have and haven't got. Use the suggestions to help you.

Have you got a kite?   Yes, I have.

- bike
- brother
- cat
- computer games
- dog
- garden
- laptop
- mobile phone
- sister

Lesson 2

There is, There are & Prepositions of Place

There is & There are

We use **there is** and **there are** to talk or ask about what exists when we are describing something in the present.
There are two mobile phones on the table.
Is there a spider in the bedroom?

We use **there is** and **there are** to describe situations and places.
There is a lizard in the garden.
There aren't any toys in the box.

Affirmative	Negative	Question	Short answers	
There's (There is)	There isn't (There is not)	Is there ...?	Yes, there is.	No, there isn't.
There are	There aren't (There are not)	Are there ...?	Yes, there are.	No, there aren't.

---

1 **Complete the sentences with There is or There are.**

1 ___There are___ two maps in the car.

2 _____ a museum in our town.

3 _____ lots of photos in my album.

4 _____ lots of sharks in the sea.

5 _____ a teddy bear on my bed.

6 _____ two puzzles in my classroom.

2 Complete the sentences with **There is, There are, There isn't** or **There aren't.**

1 ___There aren't___ any chimpanzees in the Antarctic. ✗
2 _____ some good puzzles in the toy shop. ✓
3 _____ a beautiful girl on the beach. ✓
4 _____ any lizards in the sea. ✗
5 _____ a picture of a fish in my book. ✓
6 _____ a mobile phone in the house. ✗

3 Look at the pictures and answer the questions.

1 Is there a map in the boy's hand?
___Yes, there is.___

2 Are there any books in the bag?
_____

3 Is there a robot in the shop window?
_____

4 Are there any boots under the bed?
_____

5 Is there a globe on the desk?
_____

6 Is there an astronaut on the moon?
_____

4 Complete the questions and short answers.

1 ___Are there___ any scary animals on the DVD?
No, ___there aren't___ .
2 _____ a new message on your phone?
Yes, _____ .
3 _____ any board games at school?
No, _____ .
4 _____ a toy dragon near the window?
Yes, _____ .
5 _____ any watches in the shop?
Yes, _____ .
6 _____ a guitar in your bedroom?
No, _____ .

19

Prepositions of Place

We use **prepositions of place** to show where someone or something is.

behind
The spider is behind the chair.

between
The mobile phone is between the laptop and the board game.

in
The map is in the car.

in front of
The lizard is in front of you.

near
The hut is near the beach.

next to
The skateboard is next to the bike.

on
The puzzle is on the table.

under
The box is under the table.

at	in	on
at the top	in hospital	on the left
at the bottom	in bed	on the right
at school	in the middle	on the plane
at work	in the car	on the train
at home		on the bus

5 **Look at the pictures and complete the sentences with these words.**

behind   between   in   in front of   ~~on~~   under

1 The globe is ___on___ the box.

4 The lizard is _____ the box.

2 The shoes are _____ the box.

5 The kite is _____ the box.

3 The teddy bear is _____ the box.

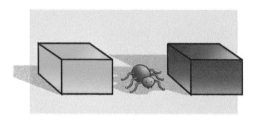

6 The spider is _____ the boxes.

6 Look at the picture and answer the questions.

1   Is there a skateboard on the table?
    No, there isn't.

2   Is there a bike under the window?
    _____

3   Are there two mobile phones behind the laptop?
    _____

4   Is there a clock between the lizard and the picture?
    _____

5   Are there any eggs in the box?
    _____

6   Is there a picture next to the door?
    _____

Speaking

Tell your partner about your bedroom. Say what there is and isn't in this room. Use prepositions of place to describe where things are in the room.

My bedroom is small, but it's got a big window. There is a desk next to the window ... .

Review 1

Units 1 & 2

1 **Complete the sentences with be.**

1 The camera ___is___ new. ✓
2 You _____ happy today. ✗
3 The astronaut _____ very tall. ✓
4 We _____ hungry. ✗
5 Mum and Dad _____ at the museum. ✗
6 I _____ crazy about computer games. ✗
7 The skateboard _____ amazing! ✓
8 It _____ warm today. ✗

2 **Complete the sentences with possessive adjectives.**

1 I've got a laptop. ___My___ laptop is cool!
2 It's Steven's birthday. _____ birthday is today.
3 You've got a mobile phone. _____ mobile phone is great.
4 We've got a rabbit. _____ rabbit is hungry.
5 There is a spider on the floor! _____ legs are very long.
6 Sam and Max have got a kite. _____ kite is in the sky!

3 **Match.**

1 Is the lizard ugly?
2 Are the chicks cold?
3 Am I funny?
4 Is Mike a good swimmer?
5 Are you a pupil?
6 Is she French?

a No, you aren't.
b Yes, he is.
c Yes, she is.
d No, I'm not.
e Yes, it is.
f Yes, they are.

4 **Look at the pictures and complete the sentences with prepositions of place.**

1 The orange is ___next to___ the apple.
2 The chair is _____ the umbrella.
3 The cats are _____ the chair.
4 The girl is _____ the tree.
5 The cat is _____ the box.
6 The yellow umbrella is _____ the green umbrella and the blue umbrella.

5 Look at the pictures and complete the sentences using the possessive 's ('s or ').

1 The _____twins'_____ presents are big.

2 The _____ teacher is short.

3 The _____ boots are old.

4 The _____ bike is new.

5 The _____ eyes are red.

6 The _____ hats are funny.

---

6 Complete the questions using **have got** and the words in brackets. Then complete the short answers.

1 ____Has the penguin got____ big feet?
(the penguin)
No, ____it hasn't____ .

2 _____ a map? (we)
Yes, _____ .

3 _____ a photo of a penguin? (Uncle Tony)
No, _____ .

4 _____ a strange pet?
(Nick and Melina)
Yes, _____ .

5 _____ an exciting job?
(you)
Yes, _____ .

6 _____ fair hair? (Lyn)
No, _____ .

7 Complete the sentences with **have got**.

1 I _____'ve got_____ a great idea! ✔

2 Sandy _____ lots of emails. ✗

3 We _____ a grey cat. ✔

4 Jason _____ dark eyes. ✔

5 You _____ a lot of homework today. ✗

6 My grandparents _____ a very beautiful garden. ✔

8 Circle the correct words.

1 There isn't / There aren't a lot of houses on the beach.

2 There are / There is three birthday presents in Kate's room.

3 Is there / Are there two teddy bears on the bed?

4 There aren't / There isn't a map of Africa in the classroom.

5 There is / There are a laptop on the desk.

6 Is there / Are there a small bottle of water in your bag?

23

Review 1

Writing Project

1 **Look at a project about sharks. Circle the correct words.**

Sharks

Sharks (1) has got / have got a bad name, people think they are scary, but most sharks (2) is not / are not dangerous.

Sharks (3) is / are a kind of fish. (4) There is / There are about 400 kinds of sharks around the world. The smallest shark, the dwarf lanternshark, is 17 centimetres long and the largest, the whale shark, (5) is / are 12 metres long.

This Caribbean reef shark can grow to about 3 metres. It (6) has got / have got big eyes, but its teeth (7) is not / are not very big. It lives close to coral reefs. (8) It's / Its favourite food is fish.

2 **Now it's your turn to do a project about an animal. Find or draw a picture of the animal and write about it.**

Present Simple Affirmative

Present Simple Affirmative

We use the **Present Simple** to talk about
* general truths.
  It snows in winter.
* things that we do regularly.
  On Sundays we go to the beach.
* permanent situations.
  My grandparents live in Spain.

We form the affirmative of the third person singular (he, she, it) by adding **-s** to the verb.

like	likes
eat	eats
give	gives

Affirmative

I sing

you sing

he sings

she sings

it sings

we sing

you sing

they sing

We form the affirmative of the third person singular of verbs that end in **–ss**, **–sh**, **-ch**, **-x** and **–o**, by adding **-es**.

miss	misses
wash	washes
touch	touches
fix	fixes
do	does

When a verb ends in a constanant + **-y**, we take off the **–y** and add **–ies** to form the affirmative of the third person singular.

study	studies
carry	carries

When a verb ends in a vowel + **-y**, we just add **-s** to form the affirmative of the third person singular.

play	plays
stay	stays

Time expressions
The following time expressions go at the beginning or at the end of a sentence: **every day/night/week/month/year, at the weekend, in the morning/afternoon/evening, on Thursdays/Saturdays**, etc.
My cousin cleans his room every Saturday.
On Wednesdays we go to my aunt's house.

1 **Complete the table.**

Verb	I/you/we/they	he/she/it
carry	carry	carries
fix		
give		
go		
like		
stay		
touch		
wash		

2 **Complete the sentences with the Present Simple. Use the verbs in brackets.**

1 In winter it _____ snows _____ in the Antarctic. (snow)
2 Matthew _____ TV in the evening. (watch)
3 Our cousins _____ with us every summer. (stay)
4 Every morning, Pat _____ his books to school. (carry)
5 Aunt Liz _____ in a museum. (work)
6 I _____ English. It's my favourite subject. (like)
7 We _____ a calculator for our maths homework. (use)
8 You _____ your car every weekend. (wash)

3 **Write sentences with the Present Simple.**

1 she / like / art
_____She likes art._____

2 on Fridays / Mark / go / to the cinema
_____

3 Maria / tidy / her room at the weekend
_____

4 I / do / my homework in my bedroom
_____

5 Natalie / know / the correct answer
_____

6 we / brush / our teeth every morning and every evening
_____

7 he / swim / in the summer
_____

8 Mr Greenhalf / teach / geography
_____

4 **Choose the correct answers.**

1 Paul and Hannah _____ in a museum.

   a work   b works

2 Kate _____ lots of fish.

   a eat   b eats

3 We _____ our pet spider at home.

   a keep   b keeps

4 Every year, you _____ me a nice present on my birthday.

   a gives   b give

5 I _____ music in my bedroom.

   a plays   b play

6 They _____ their mobile phones every day.

   a use   b uses

5 **Complete the text with the Present Simple. Use these words.**

brush	come	go	have	like	play	sit	watch

On Saturday morning, Tamsin and I (1) _____play_____ computer games. Then, we walk to the park with my dog, Trubs. Tamsin (2) _____ dogs and she's crazy about Trubs.

In the afternoon, we (3) _____ TV in my bedroom. Tamsin (4) _____ on my bed with Felicity, my cat. In the evening, Tamsin and I (5) _____ our teeth and we (6) _____ to bed.

On Sunday, Tamsin's mum (7) _____ to our house to get her.

We (8) _____ lots of fun. Tamsin is cool!

Speaking

Talk to your partner about what you do every week. Use the suggestions to help you.

> Every day I go to school.

- at the weekend
- every day
- in the morning

- in the afternoon
- in the evening
- on Mondays, Tuesdays, etc

Lesson 2

Present Simple Negative & Question

Present Simple Negative & Question

In the negative form, we use **do** or **does**, the word **not** and the infinitive of the main verb without **to** (bare infinitive).
I don't like history.
Mark doesn't wash his bike every week.

In the question form, we use **do** or **does** and the bare infinitive.
Do you eat eggs?
Does she carry her books to school?

In short answers, we only use **do** or **does**. We don't use the main verb.
Does she like my skateboard?
Yes, she does.
Do they have computer lessons?
Yes, they do.

Negative	Question	Short answers	
I don't play (do not play)	Do I play?	Yes, I do.	No, I don't.
you don't play (do not play)	Do you play?	Yes, you do.	No, you don't.
he doesn't play (does not play)	Does he play?	Yes, he does.	No, he doesn't.
she doesn't play (does not play)	Does she play?	Yes, she does.	No, she doesn't.
it doesn't play (does not play)	Does it play?	Yes, it does.	No, it doesn't.
we don't play (do not play)	Do we play?	Yes, we do.	No, we don't.
you don't play (do not play)	Do you play?	Yes, you do.	No, you don't.
they don't play (do not play)	Do they play?	Yes, they do.	No, they don't.

1 Complete the sentences with the negative form of the Present Simple. Use the verbs in brackets.

1 Max _____doesn't eat_____ spaghetti at school. (eat)

2 I _____ my teeth in the afternoon. (brush)

3 They _____ fun in the geography lesson. (have)

4 We _____ in the library. (play)

5 Sandy _____ her homework at the weekend. (do)

6 You _____ in front of the bookcase. (sit)

7 The scientist _____ a laptop. (use)

8 We _____ Japanese food. (eat)

2 Complete the questions with Do or Does. Then complete the short answers.

1 _____Does_____ she have fun at school?
No, _____she doesn't_____ .

2 _____ Tara eat hamburgers?
Yes, _____ .

3 _____ they get up at 10 o'clock on Saturdays?
Yes, _____ .

4 _____ you like eggs for breakfast?
No, _____ .

5 _____ he go to the cafeteria for lunch?
No, _____ .

6 _____ we sing in the music lesson?
Yes, _____ .

7 _____ Mrs Hanson use the globe in the geography lesson?
Yes, _____ .

8 _____ they carry their laptops to school?
No, _____ .

3 Write questions with these words. Then answer the questions so they are true for you.

1 you / wear / a uniform at school
Do you wear a uniform at school?
Yes, I do./No, I don't.

2 your best friend / like / lizards
_____
_____

3 your friends / watch / DVDs
_____
_____

4 you / have / lunch at school
_____
_____

5 your school / have a big playground
_____
_____

6 you / like / history
_____
_____

4 **Look at the pictures and answer the questions.**

1 Does he like maths?
  No, he doesn't.

2 Do they cook on Saturdays?
  _____

3 Do they wear helmets in the classroom?
  _____

4 Does she get up at 7 o'clock every morning?
  _____

5 Do the children eat in the kitchen?
  _____

6 Do you sit next to a boy in the classroom?
  _____

5 **Circle the correct words.**

1 My cousin Yoko don't / doesn't wear a helmet to school.

2 'Do you like karaoke?'
  'Yes, I do / don't.'

3 It don't / doesn't snow in the summer.

4 'Do they go to the art club after school?'
  'No, they do / don't.'

5 Mr Jones don't / doesn't teach history.

6 'Do children wear school uniforms in England?'
  'Yes, they do / does.'

7 'Does he like computer lessons?'
  'No, he don't / doesn't.'

8 We don't / doesn't eat in the cafeteria every day.

Speaking

Ask and answer questions with your partner about what you do and don't do every day. Use the suggestions to help you.

Do you have lunch at school every day?

No, I don't.

- walk to school?
- get up at 7 o'clock?
- have lunch at school?
- play in a team?
- stay home?
- meet your friends after school?

- every day
- every morning
- every afternoon
- every night
- at the weekend
- on Mondays, Tuesdays, etc

Adverbs of Frequency

Adverbs of Frequency

We use **adverbs of frequency** when we talk about habits or when we want to say how often something happens.

0% ⟷ 100%

never ⟶ sometimes ⟶ often ⟶ usually ⟶ always

Adverbs of frequency go before the main verb.
We often walk to school.
They always have lunch at 1 o'clock.

But they go after the verb **be.**
It is usually warm in the summer.
She is often at home on Wednesdays.

We use **How often ...?** to ask for more information about how often something happens.
How often do you write in your diary?
How often does mum cook spaghetti?

We can use the following time expressions to answer the question **How often ...?**
every day/week/weekend/month, once/twice/three times a day/week/month/year, etc.
How often do you cook?
Once a day.

1 **Put the words in the correct order to make sentences or questions.**

1   at / go / usually / we / to bed / 9 o'clock
    <u>We usually go to bed at 9 o'clock.</u>

2   never / Dad / works / weekend / at / the
    _____

3   ? / magazines / how often / you / read / do
    _____

4   usually / a test / have / on Tuesdays / we
    _____

5   ? / your mum / cook / how often / does
    _____

6   ? / they / how often / do / the cinema / to / go
    _____

7   your teacher / often / is / the playground / in
    _____

8   ? / go / how often / the / he / does / karaoke club / to
    _____

2 **Look at the table and complete the sentences.**

	stays home on Mondays	finishes school at 3 o'clock	wears jeans to school	reads comics in bed	talks to friends on the phone
Nicky	✓	✓ ✓ ✓ ✓	–	–	✓
Todd	✓ ✓	–	✓ ✓ ✓	✓	✓

1   Nicky _____ never _____ wears jeans to school.
2   Todd _____ reads comics in bed.
3   Todd _____ wears jeans to school.
4   Nicky and Todd _____ talk to friends on the phone.
5   Nicky _____ reads comics in bed.
6   Todd _____ finishes school at 3 o'clock.
7   Todd _____ stays home on Mondays.
8   Nicky _____ finishes school at 3 o'clock.

never –
sometimes ✓
often ✓ ✓
usually ✓ ✓ ✓
always ✓ ✓ ✓ ✓

3 **Choose the correct answers.**

1   I don't like food in the morning. I _____ have breakfast.
    (a) never   b always

2   Susie loves books. She _____ goes to the library after school.
    a never   b usually

3   I'm scared of dogs. I _____ play with them.
    a always   b never

4   Maggie likes games. She _____ buys them from the shop.
    a often   b never

5   Susie plays the guitar. She _____ goes to the music club after school.
    a sometimes   b never

6   We only do sums in the lesson. Our teacher _____ gives us sums for homework.
    a often   b never

4 Answer the questions so they are true for you. Use these adverbs of frequency.

always   never   often   sometimes   usually

1   How often do you walk to school?

_____

2   How often do you see your grandparents?

_____

3   How often do you study in the library?

_____

4   How often do you watch DVDs?

_____

5   How often do you wear jeans at school?

_____

6   How often do you talk to your friends on the phone?

_____

7   How often do you sing in the music lesson?

_____

8   How often do you have lunch at school?

_____

 **Speaking**

Ask and answer questions with your partner. Use the suggestions to help you.

> How often do you go to the beach?

> I go to the beach twice a year.

- go to the beach?
- play a sport?
- see your best friend?
- cook?
- go on holiday?
- have an English lesson?
- eat hamburgers?
- go to the cinema?

- every day
- every week
- every weekend
- every month
- once/twice/three times a day
- once/twice/three times a week
- once/twice/three times a month
- once/twice/three times a year

Question Words, Subject & Object Questions

Question Words

We use **question words** when we want more information than just **yes** or **no** in the answer.

We use the following **question words**:

* **What** to ask about things or actions.
  What is this? It's a stamp collection.
  What do you do on Saturdays? I do my homework.

* **Who** to ask about people.
  Who is this? My friend Paul.

* **Where** to ask about position or place.
  Where is my guitar? It's on your bed.

* **Whose** to ask who something belongs to.
  Whose comic is it? It's my comic.

* **When** to ask about time.
  When is the art competition? It's on Friday.

* **Why** to ask about the reason for something.
  Why do you collect stamps? I think it's interesting.

* **Which** to ask about one person or thing within a group of similar people or things.
  Which pencil do you want? I want the blue one.

* **How** to ask about the way someone does something.
  How do you go to school? I go to school by bus.

Remember!

Be careful with these words:
Who's (who is) and Whose (asks who something belongs to).
Who's in the classroom?
Clare is in the classroom.
Whose skateboard is this?
It's Clare's skateboard.

1 **Circle the correct words.**

1 What / **Who** is your favourite singer?

2 **Whose** / Who's shop is this?

3 When / **What** do you go swimming?

4 **Which** / How bag do you like?

5 Where / **What** is the matter with Donna?

6 Why / **How** do you make a kite?

7 Why / **Which** do you do your homework at school?

8 Who / **Where** is the music club?

2 Match.

1 When do you get up?
2 Where does he live?
3 Whose hamburger is this?
4 Who's the boy in school uniform?
5 What do pupils do after school?
6 How do you spell 'cat'?
7 Which ball do you want?
8 Why do you want a sandwich?

a It's George.
b The small one.
c C–A–T
d I'm hungry.
e Their homework.
f It's Nigel's.
g At half past seven.
h In a beach house.

3 Look at the pictures and complete the questions with question words.

1 _When_ is grandma's birthday? It's in March.

2 _____ is this? It's a coin.

3 _____ do you go on holiday? I usually go to Spain.

4 _____ is that lady? She's my teacher.

5 _____ present is this? It's my sister's.

6 _____ do you play computer games? I think they're exciting.

4 Put the words in the correct order to make questions.

1 the / is / Chinese lesson / when
   When is the Chinese lesson?

2 your / game / is / what / favourite
   _____

3 comics / these / whose / are
   _____

4 the puzzle / has got / who / a piece of
   _____

5 stay / in / where / you / do / the summer
   _____

6 cake / do / make / how / a / you
   _____

Subject & Object Questions

When we use **question words** to ask about the subject of a sentence (the person, animal or thing that does the action), the word order does not change and the verb stays in the affirmative form.
Who lives here?
(Sally lives here.)
Whose drink is on the table?
(Peter's drink is on the table.)

When we use **question words** to ask about the object of a sentence, then the word order changes to the question form.
What do you eat in the morning?
(I eat eggs.)
Where do you stay in the summer?
(I stay at my uncle's house.)

5 **Look at the answers and complete the subject and object questions.**

1   SQ: Who _comes from Brazil_____?
    OQ: Where _does Liz come from_____?
    Liz comes from Brazil.

2   SQ: Who _____?
    OQ: What _____?
    Tom likes puzzles.

3   SQ: What _____?
    OQ: When _____?
    The competition is on Friday.

4   SQ: Who _____?
    OQ: Where _____?
    Jamie and Helen live in Canada.

5   SQ: Whose _____?
    OQ: Where _____?
    Susan's laptop is in the classroom.

Speaking

Ask and answer the questions with your partner. Use the suggestions to help you.

Who is your best friend?

My best friend is Sally.

- What is your favourite sport?
- What is your favourite hobby?
- When is your birthday?
- What do you usually have for breakfast?
- Where do you live?

Can

Can

We use **can** to

- show ability.
  We can sing.
  Can they speak French?

- ask for or give permission to do something.
  Can I go on the ride?
  You can go to the cinema on Saturday.

Can is followed by the bare infinitive.
We use **can** for the present and the future.
Can I go on the merry-go-round now, Mum?
We can go swimming at the weekend.

We often use **can** with verbs of feeling, such as **see**, **hear**, **smell**, etc.
I can hear the roller coaster!

We don't usually use **cannot** in everyday English.
But we sometimes use it to give emphasis.
No John, you cannot go to the park!

Remember!

Bare infinitive = infinitive without to

Affirmative	Negative	Question	Short answers	
I can go.	I can't (cannot) go.	Can I go?	Yes, I can.	No, I can't.
You can go.	You can't (cannot) go.	Can you go?	Yes, you can.	No, you can't.
He can go.	He can't (cannot) go.	Can he go?	Yes, he can.	No, he can't.
She can go.	She can't (cannot) go.	Can she go?	Yes, she can.	No, she can't.
It can go.	It can't (cannot) go.	Can it go?	Yes, it can.	No, it can't.
We can go.	We can't (cannot) go.	Can we go?	Yes, we can.	No, we can't.
You can go.	You can't (cannot) go.	Can you go?	Yes, you can.	No, you can't.
They can go.	They can't (cannot) go.	Can they go?	Yes, they can.	No, they can't.

1 Complete the sentences with can or can't.

1 Teddy bears ____can't____ speak.

2 Penguins _____ swim.

3 Babies _____ ride bicycles.

4 Sharks _____ fly.

5 Spiders _____ move fast.

6 Robots _____ read magazines.

2 Complete the sentences using can or can't and the words in brackets.

1 ___Can___ he ___cook___ Chinese food? (cook)

2 Pupils _____ comics in the classroom. (read)

3 _____ we _____ to the amusement park? (go)

4 Bobby _____ a computer, because he hasn't got any money. (buy)

5 It's very cold. You _____ today. (swim)

6 We _____ lunch in the cafeteria. (have)

3 Look at the pictures and write sentences about them. Use can or can't.

1 they / play games on the computer
   They can play games on the computer.

2 the dog / come in
   _____

3 Dina / play the guitar
   _____

4 you / eat in here
   _____

5 the baby / do the puzzle
   _____

6 the girls / see the park from the ferris wheel
   _____

4 **Choose the correct answers.**

1 Where is the lizard? Oh, _____ see it now.
   a Can I   (b) I can

2 'Can Peter come with us?' '_____'
   a No, he can't.   b No, can't he.

3 Chimpanzees are clever but _____ read books.
   a can they   b they can't

4 Mum, _____ collect spiders?
   a I can   b can I

5 Keiko is Japanese. _____ speaks Japanese.
   a Can she   b She can

6 This is difficult. _____ find the answer?
   a Can you   b You can

7 'Can I have an ice cream?' '_____'
   a Yes, can you.   b Yes, you can.

8 We're too short! _____ go on that ride.
   a Can we   b We can't

5 **Write questions using can and the words in brackets.**

1 Penguins can walk. (fly)
   Can penguins fly?

2 We can play the piano. (sing)
   _____

3 Grandad can make a kite. (play computer games)
   _____

4 Robots can move. (talk)
   _____

5 You can write in your diary. (send an email)
   _____

6 Johnny can read comics. (use a calculator)
   _____

6 **Look at the picture and answer the questions.**

1 Can Mum read her book?
   Yes, she can.

2 Can the boy fly a kite?
   _____

3 Can the baby play with his toys?
   _____

4 Can the girl ride her bike?
   _____

5 Can Dad catch any fish?
   _____

6 Can the girls see any birds?
   _____

Speaking

Ask and answer questions with a partner about what you can or can't do. Use the suggestions to help you.

Can you speak English?

Yes, I can.

- make a kite
- ride a bike
- do any tricks
- use a laptop
- play the guitar
- speak Chinese
- make a cake
- play a sport

Units 3 & 4

1 **Circle the correct words.**

1 The library doesn't opens / open at 9 o'clock.

2 Dad carries / carry my baby brother to the park.

3 The children do / does their homework in the kitchen.

4 We don't / doesn't dance in the music lesson.

5 The pupils at my school reads / read lots of magazines.

6 I enjoys / enjoy art lessons.

7 Mum doesn't works / work at the weekend.

8 Our teacher tidy / tidies the classroom every afternoon.

2 **Complete the questions using the words in brackets. Then complete the short answers.**

1 _____Does it snow_____ in summer? (it / snow)   No, _____it doesn't_____ .

2 _____ a helmet to work? (Dad / wear)   Yes, _____ .

3 _____ comics at the cafeteria? (they / sell)   No, _____ .

4 _____ your kite on the beach? (you / fly)   Yes, _____ .

5 _____ ice-skating on Saturdays? (she / go)   No, _____ .

6 _____ our geography books? (we / need)   Yes, _____ .

3 **Look at the answers and complete the subject and object questions.**

1 SQ: Who _lives in Canada_____ ?
   OQ: Where _does Cathy live_____ ?
   Cathy lives in Canada.

2 SQ: What _____ ?
   OQ: When _____ ?
   The party is on Saturday.

3 SQ: Whose _____ ?
   OQ: Where _____ ?
   Mr Smith's car is in the garage.

4 SQ: Who _____ ?
   OQ: What _____ ?
   Tom wants to buy a skateboard.

5 SQ: Who _____ ?
   OQ: Why _____ ?
   Paul is sad because he has got a test.

4 **Put the words in the correct order to make sentences.**

1 her cousins / visits / Daniella / sometimes / on Saturdays
On Saturdays Daniella sometimes visits her cousins.

2 goes shopping / Susan / on Fridays / with her friends / often
_____

3 every night / takes his dog / usually / for a walk / Paul
_____

4 at the weekend / sometimes / I / ride my horse
_____

5 never / Jill / in winter / goes swimming
_____

6 play / Judy and Simone / with their doll's house / usually / after school
_____

5 Look at the pictures and complete the sentences with can or can't.

1 Tommy _____can_____ play tennis.

4 Mum _____ use a laptop.

2 Nicholas _____ speak Chinese.

5 They _____ find the sports centre.

3 My friends _____ dance.

6 Liz _____ play the piano.

6 Complete the dialogue with these words.

how   what   when   where   which   who   whose   why

Tina: Hi Lilly, (1) _____how_____ are you?

Lilly: I'm fine, thank you. Can I ring you later? I'm not at home now.

Tina: Oh, (2) _____ are you?

Lilly: I'm in a shop. I need to buy a birthday present.

Tina: (3) _____ birthday is it?

Lilly: It's Michelle's birthday tomorrow.

Tina: (4) _____ Michelle?

Lilly: My cousin Michelle.

Tina: Oh, yes! (5) _____ do you want to buy her?

Lilly: I don't know. Have you got any ideas?

Tina: (6) _____ do the shops close?

Lilly: Um, 6 o'clock I think. (7) _____ do you want to know?

Tina: Because I can come and meet you. We can buy her present together.

Lilly: Great idea! We are outside the music shop.

Tina: We? (8) _____ are you with?

Lilly: I'm with Rosie.

Tina: OK, see you soon!

Review 2

Units 3 & 4

Writing Project

1. **Look at a project about a famous building. Complete the text with these words.**

| can | can't | hear | think | usually | visit |

The Taj Mahal

Most people (1) _____think_____ of the Taj Mahal when they (2) _____ the word India. It's not surprising, it is the most famous building in India.

The Taj Mahal is a beautiful white marble building. There is a big garden around it and there is a water tank in the centre of the garden.

The Taj Mahal is one of the seven wonders of the new world. Many people (3) _____ it every year. They (4) _____ visit in October, November and February because it isn't very hot then. Visitors (5) _____ take many things into the Taj Mahal. They (6) _____ only take water, a small camera and a mobile phone.

2. **Now it's your turn to do a project about a famous building in your country. Find or draw a picture of the building and write about it.**

Imperative, Object Pronouns & Let's

Imperative

We use the **imperative** when
- we give instructions or orders.
  Cut the cake, Paul!
- we want to prevent something.
  Don't move! There's a spider over there.

We form the imperative with the bare infinitive.
We don't use a subject pronoun. The imperative is the same whether we are talking to one person or to many people.
Do your homework, Mary.
Mum, Dad, buy me some candles!
Get up! It's late.

We form the negative with the word **don't**.
Don't draw on the desk!

Remember!

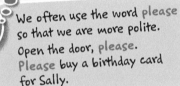

We often use the word please so that we are more polite.
Open the door, please.
Please buy a birthday card for Sally.

---

1 **Complete the sentences with the imperative. Use the verbs in brackets.**

1 _____Don't swim_____ in that water! (not swim)

2 _____ careful on the rides! (be)

3 _____ to bed. It's 12 o'clock! (go)

4 _____ that! It's paint! (not touch)

5 _____ lunch for me. I've got a sandwich. (not make)

6 _____ your teeth, please. (brush)

7 _____ there. That's my seat. (not sit)

8 _____ your books away. (put)

2 Look at the pictures and complete the sentences with the correct imperative form of these verbs.

go   drink   finish   play   ~~throw~~   write

1 _Don't throw_ the ball in the lake!

2 _____ to bed at 8 o'clock.

3 _____ in the library, please.

4 _____ your homework now.

5 _____ your name here.

6 _____ your guitar at night!

Object Pronouns

We use **object pronouns** to replace the object of a sentence. Objects are words (nouns, pronouns) that usually come after the verb.

Look at the balloons! Look at them!
Can I open the present? Can I open it?

Subject Pronouns	Object Pronouns
I	me
you	you
he	him
she	her
it	it
we	us
you	you
they	them

---

3 Complete the sentences with object pronouns.

1 Dance with ___me___, please! (I)

2 Mum made a costume for _____ . (he)

3 Throw the ball to _____ . (we)

4 Open the door for _____, please. (they)

5 Give the phone to _____ . (she)

6 Can I come shopping with _____? (you)

4 **Complete the sentences with object pronouns.**

1   Where's my uniform? I can't find ___it___ .

2   Those are my stamps. Give _____ to me!

3   I need a calculator. Find one for _____, please.

4   We're hungry. Buy two hamburgers for _____ .

5   She's a good dancer. Look at _____ .

6   They're tourists. Ask _____ where they're from.

Let's

We use **Let's** with the bare infinitive to suggest something.
Let's have lunch at Sarah's house.
Let's make a birthday cake for Nicky.

We form the negative with the word **not**.
Let's not go to the park today.
Let's not go swimming in the sea.

---

5 **Complete the sentences using Let's or Let's not and the words in brackets.**

1   ___Let's go___ to the film festival. I love films. (go)

2   _____ our bikes. It's boring. (ride)

3   _____ a party. It's your birthday! (have)

4   _____ lunch in the garden. It's cold. (have)

5   _____ our faces for the party! It's fun! (paint)

6   _____ to pop music. I don't like it. (listen)

---

6 **Match.**

1   What can we do this weekend?

2   The tourists can't speak English.

3   Those are Paul's balloons.

4   There are sharks in this sea.

5   The festival is on Saturday.

6   We need some candles for the cake.

a   Let's not swim here.

b   Let's not go to the cinema again.

c   Speak to them in French.

d   Don't give them to John.

e   Let's make something for our stall.

f   Let's get them from Dad's shop.

 **Speaking**

**Make arrangements for the weekend with
your partner. Use the suggestions to help you.**

On Saturday
morning, let's go
to the park.

OK, and on Saturday
night, let's go to
the cinema.

- watch a DVD
- go to the amusement park
- go for a walk

- have a party
- play basketball
- go bowling

Countable & Uncountable Nouns

Countable & Uncountable Nouns

Countable nouns are nouns that we can count. They have both singular and plural forms. When the subject of a sentence is in the plural, then the verb must also be in the plural.
Sam's ball is blue.
The balls are green.

Uncountable nouns are nouns that we cannot count. They don't have plural forms. When the subject of a sentence is an uncountable noun, then the verb must be in the singular.
John's got lots of work.
Ice cream is delicious.

We can use expressions such as: **a piece of, a slice of, a cup of, a glass of, a carton of, a loaf of,** etc to show how much we have of something.
I've got a piece of cake.
Two cups of coffee, please.

Remember!
We don't use *a* or *an* with uncountable nouns.

---

1 **Complete the table with these nouns.**

animal   clown   fun   hair   laptop   map   money   music   party   robot   time   work

Countable		Uncountable	
animal		fun	

2 **Look at the pictures and complete the sentences.**

1 I'm hungry. Let's make some _____*sandwiches*_____ .

2 We need red _____ for the party.

3 Dad's favourite food is _____ .

4 Sandra has got beautiful _____ .

5 Wow! That's a lot of _____ !

6 Mum, we must buy some _____ for the twins.

3 **Choose the correct answers.**

1 Our teacher always gives us _____ homework.
   a a   (b) -

2 Wow! Look at the _____ at this party!
   a food   b foods

3 This is _____ great film!
   a -   b a

4 Oh no! I've got paint in my _____ !
   a hair   b hairs

5 _____ there music at the carnival?
   a Are   b Is

6 Have you got _____ costume for the carnival?
   a -   b a

4 Look at the pictures and complete the phrases with one of these expressions.

a carton of   a cup of   a glass of   a loaf of   ~~a packet of~~   a slice of

1 _____a packet of_____ crisps

4 _____ lemonade

2 _____ milk

5 _____ bread

3 _____ pizza

6 _____ coffee

Speaking

Talk to your partner about what you've got in
- your schoolbag.
- your bedroom.

I've got lots of books in my bag.

I've got an apple and an orange.

Some & Any

It's Bonfire Night! Have you got any food for the party tonight, Clare?

Yes, I've got some food but I haven't got any drinks.

Don't worry I've got some drinks, but ...

... we haven't got any fireworks!

Some & Any

We use **some** in affirmative sentences with plural countable nouns and uncountable nouns to say that something exists.
There are some toys in the box.
There's some food in the kitchen.

We use **any** in negative sentences and questions with plural countable nouns and uncountable nouns to say that something doesn't exist or to ask if something exists.
Are there any drinks on the table?
I haven't got any homework today.

Remember!

We can use the word some in questions when we ask for or offer something.
Can I have some money, please?
Can I get you some coffee?

---

1 **Complete the sentences with some or any.**

1   I need ____*some*____ candles for the cake.

2   Have you got _____ friends in Australia?

3   There aren't _____ good costumes this year.

4   Are you hungry? We've got _____ hamburgers.

5   Are there _____ witches in the film?

6   He hasn't got _____ clues to the mystery.

7   He needs _____ money to buy Christmas presents.

8   Do you buy _____ fireworks on Bonfire Night?

9   There aren't _____ masks in the shop.

10 We need _____ food for the festival.

2 **Choose the correct answers.**

1 There aren't _____ DVDs in the room.
   a some   (b) any

2 We've got _____ lemonade in our bags.
   a any   b some

3 _____ any tickets for the play.
   a There are   b There aren't

4 Do you play _____ jokes on April Fool's Day?
   a any   b some

5 Has the clown got _____ balloons?
   a some   b any

6 _____ any kites in the shop?
   a There are   b Are there

7 Please send us _____ invitations.
   a any   b some

8 _____ any sharks in the sea.
   a There are   b There aren't

3 **Look at the pictures and complete the sentences using some or any and the words given.**

1 snow / the beach
   There isn't _____ *any snow on the beach* _____ .

2 maps / classroom
   There aren't _____ .

3 coffee / this restaurant
   Is there _____ ?

4 presents / Christmas tree
   Are there _____ ?

5 rides / amusement park
   There are _____ .

6 carnivals / Greece
   Are there _____ ?

7 food / the table
   There is _____ .

8 apples / bowl
   There are _____ .

4 Complete the dialogue with **some** or **any**.

Veronica: It's carnival time! Have you got a costume?

Grace: Yes, I have. I've got two costumes. One for me and one for you, but I haven't got (1) ___any___ hats.

Veronica: I've got (2) _____ hats. They're my brother's. We always fight about the hats and masks!

Grace: Wait, I've got an idea!

Veronica: I have, too. Let's buy (3) _____ balloons.

Grace: No, we don't need (4) _____ balloons. Dad buys them for us every year. Let's get (5) _____ paint.

Veronica: We don't need (6) _____ paint for the carnival, Grace!

Grace: Oh, yes we do. Let's throw it at your brother!

Veronica: Great idea!

Speaking

Ask and answer questions with your partner about what there is at your school. Use the suggestions to help you.

Are there any computers at your school?

Yes, there are.

- paint
- coffee
- art lessons
- lemonade
- computers
- ice cream
- balloons
- food
- comics
- cafeteria

6 Much & Many

Much & Many

We use **much** and **many** to describe quantity. We use **much** with uncountable nouns mainly in negative sentences and questions.
There isn't much cheese in my sandwich.
Have you got much time?

We use **many** with plural countable nouns mainly in negative sentences and questions.
There aren't many waiters in the restaurant.
Are there many glasses on the table?

We use **How much ...?** and **How many ...?** when we ask about quantity. We use **How much ...?** for uncountable nouns and **How many ...?** for countable nouns.
How much fruit do you eat?
How many plates are there?

Remember!

We usually don't use much and many in affirmative sentences. We use lots of or a lot of instead
She's got a lot of/lots of friends.
David drinks a lot of/lots of water.

---

1 **Circle the correct words.**

1 Are there much / **many** oranges on the tree?

2 He hasn't got **much** / many work to do today.

3 The amusment park is boring. There aren't much / **many** rides.

4 She doesn't have much / **many** snacks.

5 There aren't much / **many** desserts on the menu.

6 The man in the café hasn't got **much** / many hair.

7 Are there much / **many** children in the parade?

8 There isn't **much** / many pizza on the plate.

2 Look at the pictures and complete the sentences with much or many.

1   There isn't _____much_____ ketchup.

4   There aren't _____ drinks on this menu.

2   There aren't _____ people at the café.

5   There aren't _____ pieces in this puzzle.

3   There isn't _____ water in the glass.

6   There isn't _____ ice in this drink.

3 Complete the questions with How much or How many.

1   _____How many_____ candles are there on the cake?
2   _____ food do we need for the stall?
3   _____ glasses are there on the kitchen table?
4   _____ fast food restaurants are there in your town?
5   _____ cheese do we need for the sandwiches?
6   _____ milk do you drink in the morning?
7   _____ visitors go to the food festival every year?
8   _____ money do we need for the carnival costumes?

Speaking

Ask and answer questions with your partner about what you eat and drink. Use the suggestions to help you.

> How many meals do you have a day?

> I usually have three.

- milk / for breakfast?
- fruit / in the evening?
- meat / for dinner?

- sandwich / at school?
- water / every day?
- biscuit / every day?

A lot of, Lots of, A few & A little

A lot of, Lots of, A few & A little

We use **a lot of** or **lots of** with countable and uncountable nouns in affirmative and negative sentences and in questions.
We've got lots of food.
He hasn't got a lot of toys.
Have you got lots of friends?

We use **a few** with plural countable nouns in affirmative sentences and in questions to show that a small amount of something exists. It has a positive meaning.
She's got a few friends in China.
Do you want a few chips?

We use **a little** with uncountable nouns in affirmative sentences and in questions to show that a small amount of something exists. It has a positive meaning.
There is a little mustard.
Can I have a little juice, please?

---

1 **Choose the correct answers.**

1 They've got _____ CDs.
   a a little   (b) a lot of

2 I've got _____ good friends.
   a a few   b a little

3 There were _____ magazines on the table.
   a a little   b a few

4 For breakfast, I usually drink _____ apple juice.
   a a little   b a few

5 There's _____ food on the table.
   a a lot of   b a few

6 Suzie eats _____ meat everyday.
   a a few   b a little

7 There are _____ Indian restaurants in the city.
   a lots of   b a little

8 My brother eats _____ chicken.
   a a few   b lots of

2 **Look at the pictures and complete the sentences with a few, a little, a lot of or lots of.**

1 Nancy has got ___a lot of/lots of___ apples in her basket.

4 There are _____ eggs in the box.

2 I've got _____ chocolate.

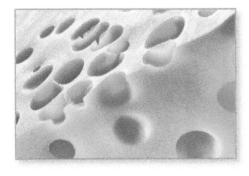

3 There are _____ holes in the cheese.

5 There's _____ juice in the glass.

6 There are _____ chips on the plate

3 **Complete the sentences with a few or a little.**

1 There's _____a little_____ milk in the glass.
2 Can I have _____ ketchup, please?
3 Let's have _____ biscuits with our orange juice.
4 Can we have _____ chips with our sandwich?
5 There are _____ knives on the table.
6 Is there _____ rice for me?
7 Matt always has _____ ham in his crepe.
8 Let's buy _____ carrots for our carrot cake.

4 **Put the words in the correct order to make sentences or questions.**

1   a few / we've / tomatoes / got
    We've got a few tomatoes.

2   coffee / want / a little / I / in / milk / my
    _____

3   ? / fish / lots of / they / do / in Spain / eat
    _____

4   for / need / a little / we / cake / the / butter
    _____

5   ? / people / are / the restaurant / in / there / a lot of
    _____

6   a little / drinks / he / with / lunch / his / juice
    _____

7   ? / children / in / a lot of / are / the / there / classroom
    _____

8   lots of / under / are / Christmas tree / there / the / presents
    _____

 **Speaking**

Talk to your partner about what you and your family buy at the supermarket. Use the suggestions to help you.

> We buy lots of fruit.

> We buy a few cakes.

- a few
- a little
- a lot of
- lots of

- apples
- bananas
- cakes
- cheese
- chicken
- chocolate

- fish
- meat
- milk
- rice
- water
- juice

Units 5 & 6

1 Complete the sentences with the imperative. Use the verbs in brackets.

1 _____Finish_____ your homework, please! (finish)

2 _____ this snack before lunch. (not eat)

3 _____ home late tonight. (not come)

4 _____ the eggs! (not forget)

5 _____ me a crepe for dinner, please. (make)

6 _____ a bottle of orange juice for the party, please. (buy)

2 Complete the sentences using **Let's** or **Let's not** and the verbs in brackets.

1 It's carnival time! _____Let's wear_____ our masks. (wear)

2 It's very cold outside. _____ skateboarding in the park. (go)

3 We've got a geography test tomorrow. _____ to the library. (go)

4 The dog is hungry. _____ it some food. (give)

5 Marco eats Italian food every day! _____ spaghetti for him. (make)

6 She's sad. _____ her a joke. (tell)

3 Complete the sentences with **some** or **any**.

1 Is there _____any_____ sugar in your tea?

2 She's got _____ fruit in her school bag.

3 Don't buy _____ ice cream. I've got lots.

4 Look! I can see _____ people in the sea!

5 I've got _____ snacks for our picnic.

6 There aren't _____ twins in my class this year.

4 Complete the sentences with object pronouns.

1 Give the knife to _____me_____, please. (I)

2 I sit next to _____ at school. (she)

3 Dad loves fireworks. We always go to Bonfire Night with _____ . (he)

4 We've got the invitations with _____ . (we)

5 Is Madeleine at the music festival with _____? (you)

6 I often send text messages to _____ . (Aunt Sue and Uncle Dave)

7 I can't find my costume for the carnival. Where is _____ ? (it)

5 Complete the questions with **How much** or **How many**.

1 _____How many_____ cartons of milk are there?

2 _____ cheese do we need for the spaghetti?

3 _____ tea does he drink every day?

4 _____ stalls are there at the festival?

5 _____ rides can you see?

6 _____ homework have we got today?

6 Circle the correct answers.

1 I want to send John - / an invitation.

2 There's a / - treasure hunt in the park today.

3 My cousin Lucy has got a / - lovely hair.

4 He's got an / - unusual coins in his collection.

5 Sam sends me an / - email every day.

6 We often eat a / - Chinese food.

7 I usually have a / - cheese sandwiches for lunch.

8 Most people really like a / - chocolate.

Units 5 & 6

7 **Complete the dialogue with these phrases.**

| a carton of | a cup of | a glass of | a jar of | a loaf of | a packet of | a slice of |

Mum: May, help me serve our visitors, please.

May: OK, Mum. What do you need?

Mum: Um, (1) _____ a cup of _____ coffee for Mr Lewis, and (2) _____ apple juice for his wife, please.

May: OK. Does Mr Lewis take milk and sugar?

Mum: Milk, yes, but no sugar. There's (3) _____ milk in the fridge.

May: Mum, let's give them (4) _____ cake, too.

Mum: Yes, you're right. There's also (5) _____ biscuits in the cupboard. Put some on a plate, please.

May: OK. Mum, I'm hungry. Have we got any sandwiches?

Mum: Well, there's (6) _____ bread on the table.

May: Great, and there's (7) _____ honey in the cupboard.

Mum: Honey sandwiches May!

May: Yes, they're delicious!

8 **Look at the pictures and choose the correct answers.**

1 There are _____ bananas at the stall.
a   lots of
b   a few

4 We've only got _____ masks for the fancy-dress party.
a   a few
b   lots of

2 There's _____ jam in the jar.
a   a little
b   a few

5 There's only _____ salad in the bowl.
a   a few
b   a little

3 There are _____ clowns at the parade.
a   a little
b   a lot of

6 There are _____ people at the carnival.
a   lots of
b   a little

Writing Project

1 **Look at a project about the Great Barrier Reef. Complete the project with these words.**

> don't   few   let's   lots   many
> remember   some   some

The Great Barrier Reef

The Great Barrier Reef is near the coast of Queensland, Australia. It is home to (1) _____ kinds of sea creatures. People from all over the world visit the reef every year.

There are over 400 kinds of coral and about 1,500 kinds of fish. (2) _____ fish can change their colours to hide from an enemy. There are also (3) _____ of different whales and dolphins. Sometimes visitors see a (4) _____ playing in the sea. These clownfish usually live in pairs. These are just (5) _____ of the animals that live on the reef.

The Great Barrier Reef is a very special place. (6) _____ protect it. (7) _____ when you visit, (8) _____ throw rubbish into the sea!

2 **Now it's your turn to do a project about a famous place in your country. Find or draw a picture of the place and write about it.**

Present Continuous Affirmative

Present Continuous Affirmative

We use the **Present Continuous** for actions that
* are in progress at the time of speaking.
  Robbie and Jake are running in the race.
* are in progress around the time of speaking.
  These days, more and more people are using the Internet.
* are temporary.
  She's living in London at the moment.

We form the affirmative with **am**, **are** or **is** and the main verb with the –**ing** ending.
read   reading
When the main verb ends in –**e**, we take off the –**e** and add –**ing**.
chase   chasing
When the verb ends in vowel + consonant, we double the final consonant and add -**ing**.
win   winning
When the verb ends in -**ie**, we take off the –**ie** and add -**y** and -**ing**.
lie   lying
When the verb ends in -**l**, we double the -**l** and add -**ing**.
travel   travelling

Time expressions
We often use the following time expressions with the **Present Continuous**: **now, at the moment, these days, this year, today, tonight**, etc.
I am writing a letter at the moment.
Monica is working a lot these days.
Simon is staying with his grandparents tonight.

Affirmative
I'm falling (I am falling)
you're falling (you are falling)
he's falling (he is falling)
she's falling (she is falling)
it's falling (it is falling)
we're falling (we are falling)
you're falling (you are falling)
they're falling (they are falling)

1 Complete the table.

fall ➡ falling	write ➡ writing	cut ➡ cutting
play	have	win
climb	dance	get
enter	leave	put
push	make	sit
sail	practise	stop
throw	ride	swim

2 Complete the sentences with the Present Continuous. Use the verbs in brackets.

1 We _____'re working_____ on the computer. (work)

2 The cat _____ the lizard. (chase)

3 Wow! Paul _____ a boat! (buy)

4 Look! Terry _____ a kite. (fly)

5 Tom _____ his bike. (fix)

6 Sally _____ the calculator. (use)

7 I _____ for my test. (study)

8 Mum and Dad _____ around Australia. (travel)

3 Complete the sentences with the Present Continuous. Use these verbs.

> do   move   run   walk   wear   write

1 I _____'m walking_____ to school today.

2 Kelly _____ new trainers.

3 The robot _____ its hands!

4 I _____ an email to Uncle Bob.

5 Wendy _____ in the race.

6 John and Bob _____ the puzzle.

4 Put the words in the correct order to make sentences.

1 are / fast / they / running / very
  They are running very fast.

2 race / Todd / entering / the / is
  _____

3 park / are / we / the / sitting / in
  _____

4 her / she / doing / is / homework
  _____

5 Mandy / are / and / volleyball / Dad / playing
  _____

6 a / having / go / Nick / is / at the moment
  _____

61

5 Look at the pictures and complete the sentences with the Present Continuous. Use these verbs.

cross   cycle   ~~drink~~   dive   give   ride   run

1 Kevin ____'s drinking____ lemonade.

4 I _____ the finish line!

2 Sheila _____ in a race.

5 Mr Jackman _____ Pete a prize.

3 Brian and Alan _____ their horses.

6 Molly and Emma _____ into the pool.

Speaking

Ask and answer questions with your partner about what the children are doing.

What is the girl under the tree doing?

She's reading a book.

Present Continuous Negative & Question

Present Continuous Negative & Question

In the negative form, we use **am, are** or **is**, the word **not** and the main verb with the –**ing** ending.
I am not working.
You are not listening.
Mel is not playing.

In the question form, we use **am, are** or **is**, and the main verb with the –**ing** ending.
Am I wearing your hat?
Are you listening to the radio?
Is Julie cooking dinner?

In short answers, we only use **am, are** or **is**. We don't use the main verb.
Am I doing my homework?
Yes, you are.
Are you enjoying the party?
No, I'm not.
Are Amanda and Paul watching TV?
Yes, they are.

Negative	Question	Short answers	
I'm not falling (am not falling)	Am I falling?	Yes, I am.	No, I'm not.
you aren't falling (are not falling)	Are you falling?	Yes, you are.	No, you aren't.
he isn't falling (is not falling)	Is he falling?	Yes, he is.	No, he isn't.
she isn't falling (is not falling)	Is she falling?	Yes, she is.	No, she isn't.
it isn't falling (is not falling)	Is it falling?	Yes, it is.	No, it isn't.
we aren't falling (are not falling)	Are we falling?	Yes, we are.	No, we aren't.
you aren't falling (are not falling)	Are you falling?	Yes, you are.	No, you aren't.
they aren't falling (are not falling)	Are they falling?	Yes, they are.	No, they aren't.

1 **Make the sentences negative.**

1 The gymnast is training.
   The gymnast isn't training.

2 She is swimming in the sea.
   _____

3 Sam and Bob are boxing.
   _____

4 I'm wearing my new jeans.
   _____

5 You are practising for the competition.
   _____

6 We're talking to the champion now.
   _____

2 **Look at the pictures and answer the questions.**

1 Is Max eating?
   Yes, he is.

2 Is the dog chasing a cat?
   _____

3 Is Tina riding a horse?
   _____

4 Are the boys bowling?
   _____

5 Is Jane playing the piano?
   _____

6 Are the boys climbing a mountain?
   _____

3 Complete the questions with the Present Continuous using the words in brackets. Then complete the short answers.

1 _____ Is she riding _____ her bike? (she / ride)

Yes, _____ she is _____ .

2 _____ a tennis match? (he / watch)

No, _____ .

3 _____ scared now? (you / feel)

No, _____ .

4 _____ in the team? (they / play)

Yes, _____ .

5 _____ the ball? (the footballer / kick)

Yes, _____ .

6 _____ to the sports centre? (we / walk)

No, _____ .

4 Complete the email with the Present Continuous. Use these verbs.

cook   do   not study   play   watch

```
● ● ○                               Email
📧 New    📧 Reply    📧 Forward    🖨 Print    🗑 Delete    📧 Send & Receive

Hi Mandy,
How are you? (1) _____ Are _____ you _____ doing _____ your homework at the moment? I (2) _____
_____ now because my sister Ginnie (3) _____ the piano and it's very
loud. Mum (4) _____ dinner and Dad (5) _____ a boxing match on TV.
Let's go to the cinema. Meet me there at 7 o'clock. There's a great film on!
Call me,
Mikey
```

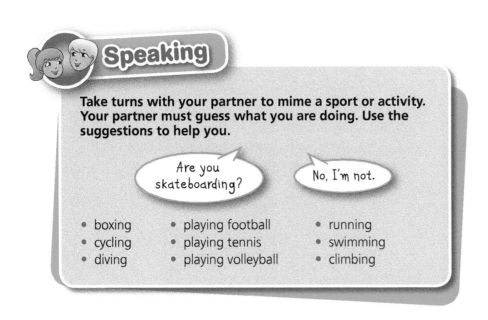

Speaking

Take turns with your partner to mime a sport or activity. Your partner must guess what you are doing. Use the suggestions to help you.

Are you skateboarding?

No, I'm not.

- boxing
- cycling
- diving
- playing football
- playing tennis
- playing volleyball
- running
- swimming
- climbing

Present Continuous (for the future)

Present Continuous (for the future)

We use the **Present Continuous** to talk about our plans for the near future.

We always use time expressions with the **Present Continuous** when we talking about the future.
I am playing in a football match on Sunday.
We are meeting at the sports centre tonight.

1 Complete the sentences with the Present Continuous. Use the verbs in brackets.

1 I _____'m washing_____ my dad's car this evening. (wash)

2 Bob _____ a guitar lesson today. (have)

3 _____ you _____ dinner tonight? (make)

4 Cathy and I _____ our grandma at the weekend. (not visit)

5 Jake and Mandy _____ in the race tomorrow. (not take part)

6 _____ Mel _____ on holiday at Christmas? (go)

7 We _____ to London this afternoon. (fly)

8 I _____ tonight. (not study)

2 Complete the letter with the Present Continuous. Use the verbs in brackets.

Hi Mum and Dad!

Summer camp is great! There are lots of things to do. This afternoon I (1) _____'m having_____ (have) a riding lesson! My friend Bob (2) _____ (come) with me. He's got a horse! This evening all the children (3) _____ (go) bowling in the village. Tomorrow morning Helen and I (4) _____ (play) tennis. It's Helen's birthday on Thursday and she (5) _____ (have) a party at the beach. Helen (6) _____ (make) a special cake for us! On Friday we (7) _____ (run) in a race in the park.

I can't wait!

See you,

Veronica

3 Look at the pictures and complete the sentences about Daniela's and Ed's plans. Use the Present Continuous.

1 On Saturday morning, Daniela _'s buying a present_____ .
2 On Saturday afternoon, Daniela _____ .
3 On Saturday afternoon, Ed _____ .
4 On Sunday morning, Daniela _____ .
5 On Sunday morning, Ed _____ .
6 On Sunday evening, Daniela and Ed _____ .

4 **Complete the dialogue with the Present Continuous. Use these verbs.**

> buy   come   go   go   have   meet   train   watch

Boy: Let's go to the sports centre one day this week. There are basketball matches every day.

Girl: OK, mm, let me think.

Boy: Can you go this afternoon?

Girl: No, I (1) _____'m going_____ mountain climbing with Dad.

Boy: Wow! That's exciting. Let's go tomorrow afternoon. There's a match at 4 o'clock.

Girl: I can't. Tomorrow afternoon I (2) _____ for the tennis competition next week. Can we go in the evening?

Boy: Oh dear. I can't. I (3) _____ the Olympic Games on TV with my family. My cousin (4) _____ at 5 o'clock.

Girl: Well, on Wednesday afternoon I (5) _____ tickets for the skating championship but I can go in the evening.

Boy: Oh, on Wednesday evening I (6) _____ my friend Clara. She's got my brother's mask and he needs it. He (7) _____ diving at the weekend.

Girl: Let's go on Thursday.

Boy: On Thursday we (8) _____ a party after school.

Girl: Yes, at three o'clock. We can go to the sports centre in the evening.

Boy: You're right. Great!

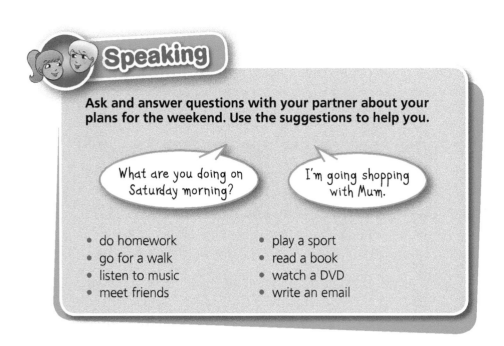

Speaking

Ask and answer questions with your partner about your plans for the weekend. Use the suggestions to help you.

> What are you doing on Saturday morning?

> I'm going shopping with Mum.

- do homework
- go for a walk
- listen to music
- meet friends
- play a sport
- read a book
- watch a DVD
- write an email

Present Simple & Present Continuous

Present Simple & Present Continuous

We use the **Present Simple** to talk about
- general truths.
  It is very hot in the desert.
- things that we do regularly.
  We go to the cinema every Saturday.
- permanent situations.
  My grandparents live in Australia.

We use the **Present Continuous** for actions that
- are in progress at the time of speaking.
  Cathy and John are playing a game.
- are in progress around the time of speaking.
  She's living in London at the moment.
- are temporary.
  My friend is working in a shop.

Remember!

We use different time expressions with the Present Simple (see page 25) and with the Present Continuous (see page 60).

1 Complete the table.

| always | at present | at the moment | every day | never | now |
| on Fridays | sometimes | this week | this year | today | usually |

Present Simple	Present Continuous
always	now

2 **Write sentences with the Present Simple and the Present Continuous.**

1 on Sundays / we / usually / have / lunch at home
but today / we / have / lunch in a restaurant
<u>On Sundays we usually have lunch at home, but</u>
<u>today we're having lunch in a restaurant.</u>
_____

4 I / usually / go / on the ferris wheel but this
afternoon / I / go / on the merry-go-round
_____
_____
_____

2 Tim / often / run / on the beach
but / today / he / run / near a castle
_____
_____
_____

5 Natalie / usually / wear / jeans
but / today /she / wear / a dress
_____
_____
_____

3 they / usually / play / volleyball at the sports centre
but this evening / they / play / in the park
_____
_____
_____

6 they / often / stay / in a cottage in summer
but / this summer / they / stay / on a houseboat
_____
_____
_____

3 **Circle the correct words.**

1 On Fridays we (don't watch)/ aren't watching much TV.
2 My family and I go / are going sailing every year.
3 Look! The cat climbs / is climbing up the tree.
4 I can't come to the sports centre now. I have / am having lunch.
5 My parents paint / are painting our new flat at the moment.
6 We don't often go / aren't often going diving on holiday.
7 Are your cousins staying / Do your cousins stay in a castle in Scotland this year?
8 We never use / are using the stairs at work.

4 **Complete the sentences with the Present Simple and the Present Continuous. Use these verbs.**

build	like	not go	not stay	ride	talk	tell	visit

1 Natasha often _____tells_____ stories about ghosts.
2 I _____ to a guard in the museum at the moment.
3 Mum _____ her job. It's near the Tower of London.
4 In winter, they _____ in their cottage by the sea.
5 Dad's in the garden now. He _____ a tree-house.
6 Every year a lot of people _____ the castle.
7 We often _____ on a boat on the River Thames.
8 Dad and Mum _____ to Uncle George's house tonight.

5 **Complete the sentences with the Present Simple and the Present Continuous. Use the verbs in brackets.**

On Friday afternoon, I (1) _____don't go_____ (not go) straight home after school. I (2) _____ (meet) my friends in the park near our school. We usually (3) _____ (play) football and sometimes we (4) _____ (ride) our bikes. We (5) _____ (have) a great time! But, today it (6) _____ (rain) so we (7) _____ (watch) a DVD at my home. We (8) _____ (eat) pizza and we (9) _____ (have) fun. My sister (10) _____ (not watch) it with us because she (11) _____ (do) her homework!

Talk to your partner about what you usually do at the weekend and what you are doing today.

On Saturday morning I usually have breakfast in the kitchen, but today I'm having breakfast in the garden.

71

Lesson 2

8 Must

Must

We use **must** to talk about
- what we have to do.
  I must go to the dentist.
- what we are obliged to do.
  I must do my homework.

Must is followed by the bare infinitive.
We use **must** for the present and the future.
I must go home, it's very late.
We must study for the test this weekend.

We use **mustn't** to talk about things we are not allowed to do.
You mustn't talk to the pilot.

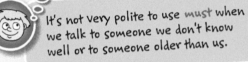

Remember!

It's not very polite to use *must* when we talk to someone we don't know well or to someone older than us.

Affirmative	Negative	Question	Short answers	
I must wash	I mustn't wash	Must I wash ...?	Yes, I must.	No, I mustn't.
you must wash	you mustn't wash	Must you wash ...?	Yes, you must.	No, you mustn't.
he must wash	he mustn't wash	Must he wash ...?	Yes, he must.	No, he mustn't.
she must wash	she mustn't wash	Must she wash ...?	Yes, she must.	No, she mustn't.
it must wash	it mustn't wash	Must it wash ...?	Yes, it must.	No, it mustn't.
we must wash	we mustn't wash	Must we wash ...?	Yes, we must.	No, we mustn't.
you must wash	you mustn't wash	Must you wash ...?	Yes, you must.	No, you mustn't.
they must wash	they mustn't wash	Must they wash ...?	Yes, they must.	No, they mustn't.

1 **Look at the pictures and complete the sentences with must or mustn't.**

1 You _____mustn't_____ touch the ball.

4 They _____ wear a uniform to school.

2 She _____ eat lots of fruit.

5 The winner _____ cross the finish line.

3 We _____ use a calculator in the test.

6 You _____ sleep in the lesson!

2 **Circle the correct answers.**

1 'Must I do my homework?' '_____'
   a Yes, you must.
   b No, you mustn't.

2 _____ eat in the museum.
   a Must visitors
   b Visitors mustn't

3 Dad's car doesn't work. _____ fix it?
   a He must
   b Must he

4 My skates are very dirty! _____ clean them for the competition?
   a Must I
   b I must

5 Sally has a test tomorrow. _____ study.
   a She must
   b Must she

6 _____ be quiet in the library. People are reading.
   a We must
   b We mustn't

7 This laptop is very expensive. _____ use it.
   a Mustn't children
   b Children mustn't

8 'Must I go to bed?' '_____'
   a Yes, you must.
   b No, you mustn't.

3 Look at the pictures about what basketball players must and mustn't do. Write questions and short answers with **must** and **mustn't**.

eat a lot of vegetables
Must they eat a lot of vegetables?
Yes, they must.

practise every day
_____
_____

drink lots of water
_____
_____

go to bed late
_____
_____

eat junk food
_____
_____

watch TV all day
_____
_____

4 Complete the telephone conversation using **must** or **mustn't** and these verbs.

buy   clean   do   eat   play   take

Mum: Ruthie, it's Mum.
Ruthie: Hi Mum!
Mum: Ruthie, we're staying with Uncle Tom this weekend. There are a few things you
(1) _____must do_____ for me.
Ruthie: OK, Mum.
Mum: First, you (2) _____ some cat food for Flopsy.
Ruthie: OK. (3) _____ I also _____ the dog for a walk?
Mum: No, Bobby can do that, but first, he (4) _____ his room. Oh, and you
(5) _____ loud music late at night.
Ruthie: Ok, Mum, bye.
Mum: Bye. Oh, and you (6) _____ all the chocolate!

Speaking

Talk to your partner about what you must or mustn't do at school.
Use the suggestions to help you.

We mustn't use mobile phones in the class.

- be early for the lesson
- be friendly to our classmates
- clean the classroom
- eat in the class
- listen to our teacher
- play jokes on the teacher
- sleep in the class
- write on the desks

Units 7 & 8

1 **Complete the sentences with the Present Continuous. Use the verbs in brackets.**

1 Nick _____'s using_____ my laptop. (use)

2 Susie _____ for the egg and spoon race! (practise)

3 Katie and Luke _____ on the beach. (lie)

4 Shh! I _____ to sleep. (try)

5 We _____ the garage door at the moment. (paint)

6 You _____ a great job! (do)

2 **Write sentences with the Present Continuous.**

1 the boys / not climb / a mountain
they / climb / a tree
The boys aren't climbing a mountain.
They are climbing a tree.

2 the children / not dance / on the beach
they / dance / at the parade
_____
_____

3 I / not buy / a salad
I / buy / a hamburger
_____
_____

4 Coach Stevens / not smile / at the players
he / shout / at them
_____
_____

5 Paul and Amanda / not cycle / on the road
they / cycle / in the park
_____
_____

6 Dad / not fix / his car
he / fix / Billy's kite
_____
_____

3 **Complete the sentences with must or mustn't.**

1 It's 11 o'clock at night. We ___mustn't___ play loud music.

2 You _____ wake up your baby sister. She's asleep.

3 I need a book for my science project. I _____ go to the library.

4 She's an athlete. She _____ eat lots of junk food.

5 Young children _____ use mobile phones.

6 He wants to win the boxing championship. He _____ practise every day.

4 **Complete the questions with the Present Continuous using the verbs in brackets. Then complete the short answers.**

1 _____Is the girl wearing_____ a helmet?
(the girl / wear)
Yes, _____she is_____ .

2 _____ paella? (you / eat)
No, _____ .

3 _____ volleyball?
(Mike and Shannon / play)
Yes, _____ .

4 _____ a picture?
(John / draw)
No, _____ .

5 _____ to the club today?
(you / walk)
Yes, _____ .

6 _____ Christmas at home this year? (we / spend)
No, _____ .

5 **Circle the correct words.**

1 Mandy **is** / are standing in front of the Crazy Mirrors.

2 He **isn't** / aren't lying on his bed at the moment.

3 **You're** / Are you chewing gum in my lesson?

4 We is / **are** making a fire to cook lunch.

5 Robin and I **am not** / aren't hiding behind the tree.

6 **They're** / Are they looking for the fast food restaurant?

Units 7 & 8

6 Complete the sentences with the Present Continuous. Use these verbs.

buy   go   make   paint   sing   spend   take

1   On Monday, Mum _____'s buying_____ me a costume for the carnival.
2   On Tuesday, Dad _____ me to the cinema.
3   On Wednesday, Mandy and I _____ in the song contest.
4   On Thursday, Mum _____ a chocolate cake.
5   On Friday, I _____ sailing with Uncle Max.
6   On Saturday, Mum and Dad _____ my room.
7   On Sunday, Mum, Dad and I _____ the day at the carnival.

7 Choose the correct answers.

1   I _____ much chocolate.
    a   don't usually eat
    b   am not usually eating

2   We _____ to Africa by plane at the moment.
    a   travel
    b   are travelling

3   They _____ early on Mondays.
    a   don't always wake up
    b   aren't always waking up

4   Mum _____ us a big breakfast at the weekend.
    a   often cooks
    b   is often cooking

5   _____ your bikes now?
    a   Do you wash
    b   Are you washing

6   Why _____ at us now?
    a   does the coach shout
    b   is the coach shouting

8 Complete the dialogue with the Present Simple or the Present Continuous. Use these verbs.

do   help   practise   study   take part   wash

Nell: Hi Josh, how are you?
Josh: I'm fine, and you?
Nell: I'm fine, Josh. What (1) _____are you doing_____?
Josh: Oh, I (2) _____ for the cycling race. It's tomorrow.
Nell: That's exciting.
Josh: Yes, it is. My sister and I (3) _____ in the race every year but this
          year she can't. She's got a test on Monday, so she (4) _____ at
          the moment.
Nell: I see. I always (5) _____ Dad on Saturdays. At the moment, we
          (6) _____ the cars. Boring!
Josh: Mm. Hey, come and watch me in the race!
Nell: Yes, that's a great idea! See you tomorrow.

1 **Look at a project about a popular activity. Circle the correct words.**

Camping

Camping (1) is / is being a very popular activity all around the world. People can relax, forget about school and work and enjoy nature. Many children and adults (2) go /are going camping every year.

This family (3) camps / is camping by the sea. They (4) don't sleep / aren't sleeping. They (5) sit / are sitting around the fire. They (6) enjoy / are enjoying the view. It's a lovely place, but they (7) must be / must being careful because the sea can be dangerous. They (8) mustn't sit / mustn't be sitting too close to the edge.

2 **Now, it's your turn to write about a popular activity. Find or draw a picture of the activity and write about it.**

Past Simple: Be, There was & There were

> Where's Dad? He was here five minutes ago.

Past Simple: Be

The **Past Simple** of the verb **be** is **was** and **were**. We use the **Past Simple** for events, situations and habits in the past.
The party was great fun.
The children were very quiet.

In the negative form, we add the word **not** after **was** or **were**.
The boys weren't scared.
Mandy wasn't at school.

In the question form, we use **was** or **were**.
Was the train ride interesting?
Were the camels in the desert?

Time expressions
We often use the following time expressions with the **Past Simple**, they go at the end or at the beginning of a sentence: **yesterday, yesterday morning/afternoon, last night/week/month/year, two hours/days/weeks ago,** etc.
I was at home last night.
Last month Mum and Dad were on holiday.

Affirmative	Negative	Question	Short answers	
I was	I wasn't (was not)	Was I ...?	Yes, I was.	No, I wasn't.
you were	you weren't (were not)	Were you ...?	Yes, you were.	No, you weren't.
he was	he wasn't (was not)	Was he ...?	Yes, he was.	No, he wasn't.
she was	she wasn't (was not)	Was she ...?	Yes, she was.	No, she wasn't.
it was	it wasn't (was not)	Was it ...?	Yes, it was.	No, it wasn't.
we were	we weren't (were not)	Were we ...?	Yes, we were.	No, we weren't.
you were	you weren't (were not)	Were you ...?	Yes, you were.	No, you weren't.
they were	they weren't (were not)	Were they ...?	Yes, they were.	No, they weren't.

1 Complete the sentences with was or were.

1 The camels _____ were _____ thirsty.
2 There _____ lots of people at summer camp.
3 The hot dog _____ delicious.
4 The swimsuit _____ in Mum's suitcase.
5 We _____ in the tent last night.
6 Jake _____ in front of the pyramids.
7 Our passports _____ on the table.
8 I _____ at the beach last Saturday.

2 Make the sentences negative.

1 The skiing holiday was fun.   The skiing holiday wasn't fun. _____
2 The girls were scared of the spiders.   _____
3 The camel ride was exciting.   _____
4 I was very hungry this morning.   _____
5 Mel and Kim were in India a month ago.   _____
6 We were in the Sahara Desert last week.   _____

3 Complete the questions with Was or Were. Then write short answers.

1 ____ Was ____ the camel very tall? ✓
   Yes, it was. _____

2 _____ the old buildings in the city centre? ✗
   _____

3 _____ the music too loud? ✓
   _____

4 _____ you at the Tower of London yesterday? ✗
   _____

5 _____ the masks cheap? ✗
   _____

6 _____ Shelley in Australia last month? ✓
   _____

7 _____ I the winner? ✗
   _____

8 _____ the magician on the train? ✓
   _____

There was & There were

The Past Simple of **there is** and **there are** is **there was** and **there were**. We use **there was** and **there were** to talk or ask about something that existed in the past.
There was a lot of food on the table.
There were three spiders in the tent.

Affirmative	Negative	Question	Short answers	
There was	There wasn't (There was not)	Was there ...?	Yes, there was.	No, there wasn't.
There were	There weren't (There were not)	Were there ...?	Yes, there were.	No, there weren't.

4 **Complete the sentences with** There was, There were, There wasn't **or** There weren't.

1 ___There were___ many tourists on the beach. ✓

2 _____ much snow on the mountain. ✗

3 _____ any umbrellas in the sand. ✗

4 _____ many people on the plane. ✓

5 _____ a sailing boat in the sea. ✓

6 _____ two swimming pools at the hotel. ✓

5 **Circle the correct words.**

1 Mum and Dad wasn't / weren't on the houseboat last weekend.

2 Was / Were the hotel expensive?

3 There was / were a lot of people at the parade.

4 There were / Were there any snakes in the desert?

5 My trainers was / were under the suitcase!

6 Sally was / were in France last week.

7 Was / Were you at the cycling race this morning?

8 The mountain bike wasn't / weren't cheap!

6 **Look at the picture and complete with** was, wasn't, were **or** weren't.

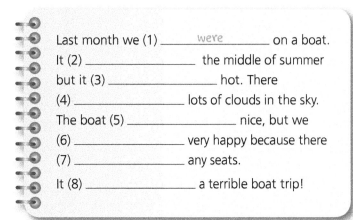

Last month we (1) _____were_____ on a boat.
It (2) _____ the middle of summer
but it (3) _____ hot. There
(4) _____ lots of clouds in the sky.
The boat (5) _____ nice, but we
(6) _____ very happy because there
(7) _____ any seats.
It (8) _____ a terrible boat trip!

Think about your holiday last year. Ask and answer the following questions with your partner.

• Was it a summer or a winter holiday?
• Were you with your family?
• Were your friends with you?
• Were you at the beach, in the mountains or in the countryside?
• Was it boring or interesting?

Past Simple Affirmative: Regular Verbs

Last summer, Sandy was in Athens.
She visited the Acropolis, ...

... and some museums.

She walked in the town and shopped for
presents for her family, ...

... and then she relaxed in her hotel room.

Past Simple Affirmative: Regular Verbs

We use the **Past Simple** for
- actions or situations which started and finished in the past.
  We stayed in a hotel on the beach.
- past habits.
  Mum and Dad travelled a lot.
- actions which happened one after the other in the past.
  He washed his face, brushed his teeth and walked down the stairs.

We form the affirmative of regular verbs by adding the **-ed** ending.
want   wanted

Affirmative

I watched
you watched
he watched
she watched
it watched
we watched
you watched
they watched

When the verb ends in **–e**, we just add **–d**.
use   used

When the verb ends in a consonant + **-y**, we take off the **–y** and add **–ied**.
try   tried

When the verb ends in a vowel + **-y**, we just add **-ed**.
stay   stayed

When the verb ends in vowel + consonant, then we double the last consonant and add **-ed**.
fit   fitted

When the verb ends in **-l**, we double the **-l** and add **-ed**.
travel   travelled

Time Expressions
The following time expressions are used with the **Past Simple: yesterday, last night/week/month/year**, etc.
They travelled to Japan last year.

Ago
We use **ago** to talk about something that happened a number of years, minutes, days, etc in the past.
I arrived ten minutes ago.
She visited Egypt three years ago.

1 **Complete the tables.**

Verb	Past Simple
carry	carried
chase	
cry	
fit	
look	
start	

Verb	Past Simple
stay	stayed
tie	
travel	
try	
want	
use	

2 **Complete the sentences with the Past Simple. Use the verbs in brackets.**

1 The children _____played_____ Monopoly after dinner. (play)
2 Amanda's new jeans _____ her well. (fit)
3 The flight _____ at 6 o'clock. (land)
4 I _____ in a flat near the River Thames. (live)
5 The passengers _____ their tickets and passports. (need)
6 John _____ the bags into the house. (carry)
7 Paul _____ the book about lizards. (like)
8 Susan _____ her swimsuit. (wash)
9 The bus _____ at the Eiffel Tower. (stop)
10 Uncle Jim _____ on a big ship. (work)

3 **Complete the text with the Past Simple. Use these verbs.**

arrive   dance   decide   enjoy   stay   travel   try   visit

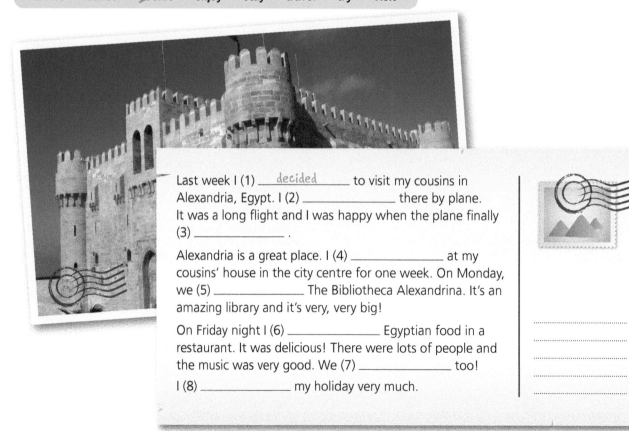

Last week I (1) _____decided_____ to visit my cousins in Alexandria, Egypt. I (2) _____ there by plane. It was a long flight and I was happy when the plane finally (3) _____ .

Alexandria is a great place. I (4) _____ at my cousins' house in the city centre for one week. On Monday, we (5) _____ The Bibliotheca Alexandrina. It's an amazing library and it's very, very big!

On Friday night I (6) _____ Egyptian food in a restaurant. It was delicious! There were lots of people and the music was very good. We (7) _____ too!

I (8) _____ my holiday very much.

4 **Look at the pictures and complete the sentences with the Past Simple. Use these verbs.**

carry   climb   cook   count   open   ~~try~~   wait   watch

1 Susie ___tried___ the apple juice.

5 My cat Mindy _____ up the tree.

2 Dad _____ our suitcases to the port.

6 Nick _____ all his presents after the party.

3 We _____ the planes at the airport.

7 The coach _____ his players.

4 Dan and Mandy _____ at the bus stop this afternoon.

8 My Mum _____ spaghetti for dinner last night.

Speaking

Talk to your partner about the following things.

I played Monopoly last night.

I talked to my best friend last night.

- something you watched on TV
- a game you played
- a person you talked to
- somewhere you visited
- a film you enjoyed

Past Simple Affirmative: Irregular Verbs

Past Simple Affirmative: Irregular Verbs

There are lots of irregular verbs in English. Irregular verbs do not follow the rules on page 81. We form the Past Simple of irregular verbs in different ways. See the Irregular verbs list on page 113.

1 Complete the tables.

Verb	Past Simple
bring	brought
catch	
come	
fall	
feel	
give	
hold	
keep	

Verb	Past Simple
know	knew
put	
ride	
run	
sell	
think	
throw	
win	

2 **Complete the sentences with the Past Simple. Use the verbs in brackets.**

1 We _____found_____ a beautiful shell in the sand. (find)

2 Mum and Dad _____ a new tent for our camping trip. (buy)

3 I _____ lots of delicious pizza in Rome. (eat)

4 Cindy _____ a photo of the diving champion! (take)

5 They _____ many tall buildings in New York. (see)

6 Oh no! I _____ my sun cream at home. (leave)

7 You _____ a beautiful dress to the party. (wear)

8 Johnny _____ a wonderful time in Portugal. (have)

3 **Look at the pictures and complete the sentences with the Past Simple. Use these verbs.**

cut   break   draw   leave   read   write

1 Georgina _____drew_____ a beautiful picture.

4 Veronica _____ her birthday cake.

2 Nicholas _____ his leg on holiday.

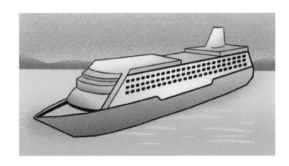

5 The ship _____ the port two hours ago.

3 I _____ a really interesting book yesterday.

6 You _____ a really interesting story.

85

4 Complete the diary with the Past Simple. Use these verbs.

| be | be | choose | drink | fly | go | have | make | meet | sit | swim | take |

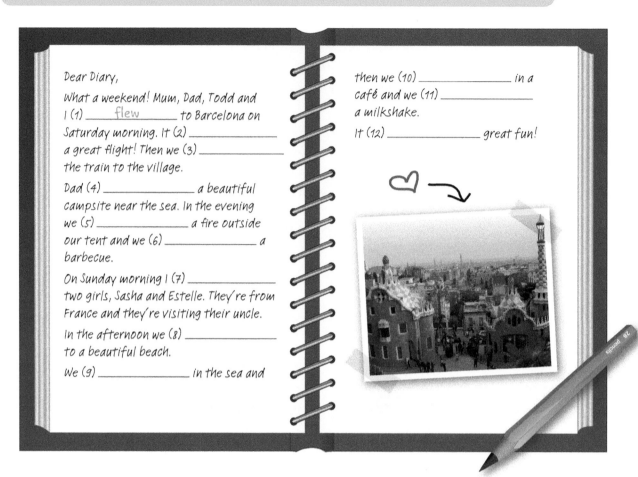

Dear Diary,

What a weekend! Mum, Dad, Todd and I (1) _____flew_____ to Barcelona on Saturday morning. It (2) _____ a great flight! Then we (3) _____ the train to the village.

Dad (4) _____ a beautiful campsite near the sea. In the evening we (5) _____ a fire outside our tent and we (6) _____ a barbecue.

On Sunday morning I (7) _____ two girls, Sasha and Estelle. They're from France and they're visiting their uncle.

In the afternoon we (8) _____ to a beautiful beach.

We (9) _____ in the sea and

then we (10) _____ in a café and we (11) _____ a milkshake.

It (12) _____ great fun!

Speaking

Talk to your partner about a holiday you enjoyed. Say where you went, who you went with, how you travelled there and what you did there.

I went to China in July.

Who did you go with?

Past Simple Negative & Question: Regular & Irregular Verbs

Past Simple Negative & Question: Regular & Irregular Verbs

In the negative form, we use **did**, the word **not** and the bare infinitive.
She didn't go to the film studio.
We didn't enjoy the concert.

In the question form, we use **did** and the bare infinitive.
Did you get his autograph?
Did they give her the role?

In short answers, we use **did** or **didn't**. We don't use the main verb.
Did Alan buy a puzzle?
Yes, he did.
Did Lyn and Caroline go the party?
No, they didn't.

Negative	Question	Short answers	
I didn't come (did not come)	Did I come ...?	Yes, I did.	No, I didn't.
you didn't come (did not come)	Did you come ...?	Yes, you did.	No, you didn't.
he didn't come (did not come)	Did he come ...?	Yes, he did.	No, he didn't.
she didn't come (did not come)	Did she come ...?	Yes, she did.	No, she didn't.
it didn't come (did not come)	Did it come ...?	Yes, it did.	No, it didn't.
we didn't come (did not come)	Did we come ...?	Yes, we did.	No, we didn't.
you didn't come (did not come)	Did you come ...?	Yes, you did.	No, you didn't.
they didn't come (did not come)	Did they come ...?	Yes, they did.	No, they didn't.

1 **Complete the sentences with the negative form of the Past Simple. Use the verbs in bold.**

1 I **got** the singer's autograph, but I _____didn't get_____ the actor's.
2 Mary **saw** her favourite pop group, but she _____ Madonna.
3 Max and Sam **went** to the amusement park, but they _____ to the cinema.
4 Mel and I **bought** some hamburgers, but we _____ any chips.
5 Mark **liked** the songs, but he _____ the books.
6 The cat **played** with the mouse, but it _____ with the dog.

2 **Make the sentences negative.**

1 She wanted the role.
   She didn't want the role.

2 The audience enjoyed the concert.
   _____

3 He went for an interview.
   _____

4 We found the film studio.
   _____

5 They agreed to shoot a film.
   _____

6 The cameraman looked happy.
   _____

3 **Change the sentences into questions.**

1 You met a famous scientist.
   Did you meet a famous scientist?

2 They talked to the dancer.
   _____

3 You travelled by boat.
   _____

4 She took part in the competition.
   _____

5 We forgot the tickets.
   _____

6 The magician did lots of tricks.
   _____

4 **Look at the pictures and complete the questions using these verbs. Then write short answers.**

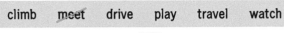

climb ~~meet~~ drive play travel watch

1 ___Did___ Sam ___meet___ a famous tennis player?
   ___Yes, he did.___

4 _____ the boys _____ the volleyball match?
   _____

2 _____ Dina _____ the guitar at the concert?
   _____

5 _____ Paul _____ the mountain?
   _____

3 _____ the family _____ by train?
   _____

6 _____ you _____ to work?
   _____

Speaking

Ask and answer questions with your partner about what you did and didn't do last week. Use the suggestions to help you.

Did you go to the park?

Yes, I did.

- go to the cinema
- see a film
- buy CDs
- listen to the radio
- go to a concert
- get a famous person's autograph
- take photos
- have a test

10

Question Words with the Past Simple

Question Words with the Past Simple

We use question words with the **Past Simple** to find out more information about an action in the past.

Who broke the glass? (Jane broke the glass.)
What did Jane break? (Jane broke a glass.)
When did Jane break the glass? (She broke it yesterday.)
Where did Jane break it? (She broke it in her bedroom.)
Which glass did she break? (She broke the blue one.)
Whose glass was it? (It was her mum's.)
How did she break it? (She dropped it.)

Remember!

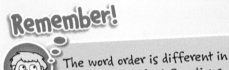

The word order is different in Subject and Object Questions.
Who bought a toy?
(Mandy bought a toy.)
What did Mandy buy?
(Mandy bought a toy.)

---

1 **Complete the dialogue with question words.**

Helen: (1) _____What_____ did you do on Saturday night, Henry?

Henry: I went to the cinema.

Helen: Oh, (2) _____ film did you see?

Henry: I saw a horror film but I didn't like it.

Helen: (3) _____ didn't you enjoy it?

Henry: Well, it wasn't scary! (4) _____ did you spend your Saturday night, Helen?

Helen: I went to the pop concert.

Henry: Oh, (5) _____ did you go with?

Helen: My cousins.

Henry: Did you have fun at the concert?

Helen: Yes, I did.

Henry: (6) _____ songs did the pop group sing?

Helen: Lots of songs. All amazing, of course!

2 Circle the correct words.

1 Where they shot / did they shoot the romance?

2 Whose story the children enjoyed / did the children enjoy?

3 How you found / did you find tickets to the new musical?

4 Who thought / did they think the adventure film was exciting?

5 When she started / did she start acting?

6 Whose bike rode Jane / did Jane ride?

7 Why he ate / did he eat your hotdog?

8 Who you saw / did you see the western with?

3 Write questions with the Past Simple about the underlined words. Use these question words.

how   what   when   where   who   why

1 _When did the dancer arrive?_

The dancer arrived <u>yesterday</u>.

2 _____

They travelled to Italy <u>by boat</u>.

3 _____

She visited <u>her aunt</u> in Ireland.

4 _____

The actor stayed <u>in a hotel</u>.

5 _____

She missed <u>the new action film</u>.

6 _____

She smiled <u>because she got the role</u>.

4 Write questions with the Past Simple.

1 who / they / give / the award to
  Who did they give the award to?

2 which / actor / Thomas / speak to

  _____

3 who / he / sell / the company to

  _____

4 how / I / lose / my laptop

  _____

5 where / Jake / see a ghost

  _____

6 which medal / the champion / win

  _____

7 why / the cameraman / shout

  _____

8 when / you / have / a riding lesson

  _____

Imagine that you went somewhere and you met a famous person. Ask and answer questions about this person with your partner.

Who did you meet?

I met Justin Timberlake.

• Who did you meet?
• When did you meet him or her?
• Where did you meet him or her?
• Why did you go there?
• How did you get there?
• What did he or she say to you?

91

Review 5

Units 9 & 10

1 Choose the correct answers.

1 The western film _____ very exciting.
   - (a) was
   - b were

2 The children _____ from Japan.
   - a wasn't
   - b weren't

3 My flight _____ long.
   - a was
   - b were

4 I _____ at the film studio yesterday.
   - a wasn't
   - b weren't

5 Hannah _____ late for school this morning.
   - a was
   - b were

6 We _____ at the hotel last night.
   - a wasn't
   - b weren't

2 Look at the pictures and complete the sentences with There was, There were, There wasn't or There weren't.

_____There was_____ lots of snow last winter.

_____ lots of clothes in the suitcase.

_____ many cruise ships in the port.

_____ a young woman at the bus stop.

_____ any trees in the desert.

_____ any money in the purse.

3 Complete the sentences with the Past Simple. Use the verbs in brackets.

1 Two years ago we _____stayed_____ in a beautiful hotel in London. (stay)

2 I _____ my school bag to school. (carry)

3 Sharon _____ to work by train this morning. (travel)

4 The boys _____ us in the playground. (chase)

5 You're late! The lesson _____ at 9 o'clock. (start)

6 My parents and I _____ the Eiffel Tower last year. (visit)

7 We _____ a trick on my dad last week! (play)

8 John _____ the film last night. (enjoy)

4 **Look at the pictures and write questions using the Past Simple and the words given. Then write short answers.**

1

Oliver / break a window
Did Oliver break a window?
No, he didn't.
_____

4

the family / drive to the airport
_____
_____
_____

2

Sally and Ann / run on the beach
_____
_____

5

Paula / take a picture of some penguins
_____
_____

3

Mr Baker / buy a skateboard
_____
_____

6

Bill and Mandy / have a picnic
_____
_____
_____

5 **Complete the table.**

Verb	Past Simple
go	went
come	
break	
find	
give	
know	
see	
think	

6 **Make the sentences negative. Use the words in brackets.**

1 Jill and Mark walked a lot in Paris. (London)
They didn't walk a lot in London.

2 I enjoyed the musical. (film)
_____

3 Mum took us to the cinema last week. (theatre)
_____

4 Steven left his laptop on the plane. (suitcase)
_____

5 You played tennis yesterday. (basketball)
_____

6 The dog ate my biscuit! (cake)
_____

7 **Write questions with the Past Simple about the underlined words. Use these question words.**

| How | What | When | Where | Who | Why |

1 When did you go on a cruise?
I went on a cruise last week.

2 _____
They visited the pyramids.

3 _____
I saw my teacher at the airport.

4 _____
We left our passports at home!

5 _____
She chose Spanish because she loves Spain.

6 _____
He travelled to Ireland by train.

93

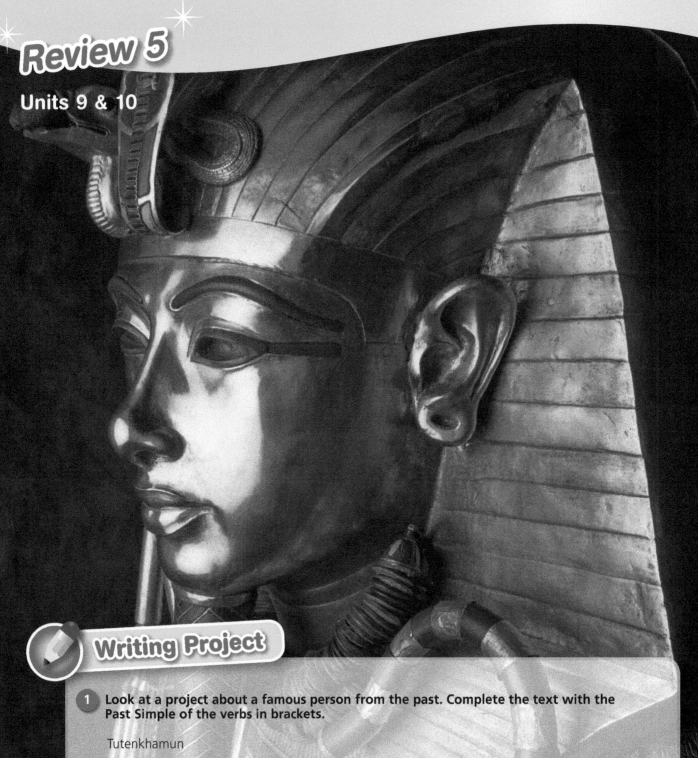

Review 5

Writing Project

1 Look at a project about a famous person from the past. Complete the text with the Past Simple of the verbs in brackets.

Tutenkhamun

Tutenkhamun (1) ___was___ (be) the youngest king of Egypt. He was eight or nine years old when he (2) _____ (become) pharaoh. He was about nineteen when he (3) _____ (die).

Howard Carter (4) _____ (discover) Tutenkhamun's tomb in 1922. The mummy of the young Egyptian king was inside a beautiful gold coffin. The tomb was amazing. It was full of gold. There (5) _____ (be) also lots of other beautiful things inside.

The pharaohs of Ancient Egypt (6) _____ (want) to take their treasure into the next life, so they (7) _____ (fill) their tombs with beautiful things.

How (8) _____ (Tutenkhamun / die)? Many people (9) _____ (try) to find the answer, but it is still a mystery.

2 Now it's your turn to do a project about a famous person from your country's past. Find or draw a picture of the person and write about him or her.

Comparative

Comparative

We use the **comparative** to compare two people, animals or things. We often use the word **than** after the **comparative**.
Our cat is smaller than our dog.
An elephant is bigger than a tiger.

Short adjectives

* We add **-er** to adjectives with one syllable.
  long   longer
* When the adjective ends in **-e**, we just add **-r**.
  close   closer
* When the adjective ends in vowel + consonant, we double the last consonant and add **-er**.
  big   bigger
* When the adjective ends in **-y**, we take off the **-y** and add **-ier**.
  pretty   prettier

Long adjectives

* We form the comparative of two-syllable adjectives by using the word **more** before the adjective.
  boring   more boring
* Some two-syllable adjectives have two comparative forms.
  clever   cleverer or more clever
* We form the comparative of adjectives with three or more syllables by using the word **more** before the adjective.
  exciting   more exciting

Irregular adjectives

There are irregular adjectives, which do not follow these rules.

good   better
bad   worse
far   further or farther

The words **much, many, a lot of, lots of, a little** and **a few** also have a comparative form.

much	*more*		*lots of*	*more*
many	*more*		*a little*	*less*
a lot of	*more*		*a few*	*fewer*

95

1 Complete the tables.

Adjective	Comparative
big	bigger
fast	
far	
good	
high	
horrible	
hot	
interesting	
pretty	
serious	

Adjective	Comparative
amazing	more amazing
bad	
beautiful	
boring	
close	
dangerous	
exciting	
happy	
hard	
long	

2 Complete the sentences with the comparative form of the adjectives in brackets.

1   Egypt is _____hotter_____ than England. (hot)

2   Paul is _____ than his brother. (lazy)

3   My binoculars are _____ than Teddy's. (expensive)

4   The road is _____ than the path. (wide)

5   The orange butterfly is _____ than the blue one. (small)

6   Kathy's science mark is _____ than mine. (bad)

7   Simon is _____ than Henry. (intelligent)

8   Kate's hair is _____ than mine. (short)

9   The lake is _____ than the river. (clean)

10   John's house is _____ away than mine. (far)

3 Complete the sentences with the comparative form of these adjectives.

~~cheap~~   cold   fast   good   heavy   small

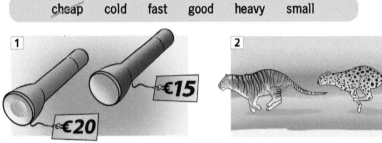

The red torch is ____cheaper____ than the blue torch.

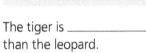

The tiger is _____ than the leopard.

The blue fish is _____ than the pink one.

The elephant is _____ than the pig.

John's drawing is _____ than Paul's.

The penguin's home is _____ than the lion's.

4 **Complete the sentences. Use** as ... as **and** not as ... as.

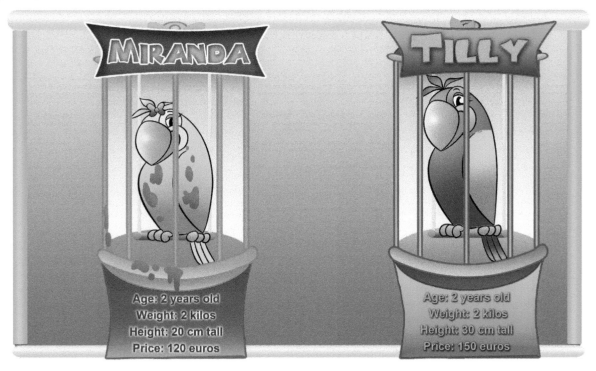

1 Miranda is _____ *as old as* _____ Tilly. (old)
2 Miranda is _____ Tilly. (tall)
3 Miranda is _____ Tilly. (heavy)
4 Miranda is _____ Tilly. (clean)
5 Miranda is _____ Tilly. (expensive)

 **Speaking**

Use the comparative form and talk about pets with your partner. Use the suggestions to help you.

Cats are nicer than dogs.

Dogs are friendlier than rabbits.

- cat
- dog
- mouse
- spider
- rabbit
- lizard
- friendly
- good
- horrible
- nice
- sweet
- tiny

Superlative

Superlative

We use the **superlative** to compare more than two people, animals or things. We use the word **the** before the **superlative**.
We often use a phrase beginning with **in** or **of** to continue the sentence.
Russia is the biggest country in the world.
Elena is the quietest student in the class.

Short adjectives

* We add **–est** to adjectives with one syllable.
  kind   the kindest
* When the adjective ends in **–e**, we just add **–st**.
  nice   the nicest
* When the adjective ends in vowel + consonant, we double the last consonant and add **–est**.
  big   the biggest
* When the adjective ends **–y**, we take off the **–y** and add **–iest**.
  ugly   the ugliest

Irregular adjectives

There are irregular adjectives, which do not follow these rules.
good   the best
bad   the worst
*far   the furthest **or** the farthest*

Long adjectives

* We form the superlative of two-syllable adjectives by using the words **the most** before the adjective.
  boring   the most boring
* Some two-syllable adjectives have two superlative forms.
  *clever   the cleverest **or** the most clever*
* We form the superlative of adjectives with three or more syllables by using the words **the most** before the adjective.
  amazing   the most amazing

The words **much, many, a lot of, lots of, a little** and **a few** also have a superlative form.

much	*the most*	*lots of*	*the most*
many	*the most*	*a little*	*the least*
a lot of	*the most*	*a few*	*the fewest*

98

1 Complete the table.

Adjective	Comparative	Superlative
bad	worse	the worst
difficult	more difficult	
easy	easier	
good	better	
hard	harder	
hot	hotter	
important	more important	
many	more	
popular	more popular	
strange	stranger	

2 Complete the sentences with the superlative form of the adjectives in brackets.

1 My puppy is _____the noisiest_____ pet in the neighbourhood! (noisy)

2 Helen's pony is _____ of all! (fast)

3 I went to _____ carnival last week. (boring)

4 We saw _____ peacock at the zoo. (amazing)

5 The goldfish was _____ fish in the bowl. (small)

6 James is _____ boy in our class. He's got a pet mouse! (lucky)

7 Last week I came first in the horse-riding competition. It was _____ day of my life! (exciting)

8 _____ thing about my uncle's farm is the insects. (horrible)

3 Complete the dialogue with the superlative form of the adjectives in brackets.

Richie: Hi, Maggie. Did you enjoy your birthday party?

Maggie: Yes, I did.

Richie: It was (1) _____the best_____ (good) party this year.

Maggie: Yes, it was. The clowns were wonderful. Max was (2) _____ (funny) clown and he did some amazing tricks.

Richie: Yes, he did and we played some great games. The food was nice, too. I loved the hamburgers and pizza, but the hotdogs were (3) _____ (tasty).

Maggie: Yes, they were. Mum and Dad got me (4) _____ (unusual) present.

Richie: What did they get you?

Maggie: A parrot. It says (5) _____ (silly) things and it's got (6) _____ (beautiful) colours.

Richie: Oh, I love parrots!

HAPPY Birthday

4 **Look at the pictures and complete the sentences with the superlative form of these adjectives.**

big   lazy   ~~long~~   many   small   slow   strong   young

1   The monkey has got _the longest_ tail.

2   The white cat is _____ cat. It wakes up at 8 o'clock!

3   The lion is _____ animal.

4   The white mouse is _____ .

5   The tortoise is _____ animal in the race.

6   Africa has got _____ elephants in the world.

7   The dinosaur's egg is _____ .

8   Tim's dog is _____ !

Use the superlative form to talk about the picture of a farm with your partner.
Use the suggestions to help you.

The black dog is the fastest.

The grey rabbit is the fattest.

- big / small
- clean / dirty
- fast / slow
- fat / thin
- tall / short
- old / young

Comparative & Superlative

Comparative & Superlative

We use the **comparative** to compare two people, animals or things.
We often use the word **than** after the comparative.
The cat is bigger than the mouse.

as ... as
We can also use **as** + adjective + **as** to compare two people, animals
or things. We use **as ... as** when the two people, animals or things are
the same. We use **not as ... as** when the two people, animals or things
are not the same.
This computer game is as expensive as that one.
English is not as difficult as Japanese.

We use the **superlative** to compare more than two people, animals or
things. We use the word **the** before the superlative. We often use a
phrase beginning with **in** or **of** to continue the sentence.
The giraffe is the tallest animal in the world.

Remember!

See the rules for comparative and superlative forms on pages 95 & 98.

---

1 **Circle the correct words.**

1 Erica's dog is friendlier / the friendliest than Sam's.

2 Peter's house is bigger than / the biggest in the street.

3 I have got most / more books than you.

4 Carla is cleverer / the cleverest than her brother.

5 The maths test was easier / the easiest than the geography test.

6 Joanne is the best / better than student in my class.

7 This peacock has got brighter / the brightest colours than that peacock.

8 Our cat sleeps inside at night because it's warmer / the warmest than the garden.

2 **Choose the correct answers.**

1 Monkeys are _____ worms.
   a the most clever
   (b) more clever than

2 My binoculars are _____ as the scientist's.
   a as good
   b better than

3 The zoo is _____ the park.
   a the furthest
   b further than

4 The cave at the end of the beach is _____ of all.
   a scarier than
   b the scariest

5 Fish is _____ meat.
   a healthier than
   b the healthiest

6 The pirate costume is _____ than the cowboy's.
   a more popular
   b the most popular

7 Chimpanzees are not _____ as lions.
   a more dangerous
   b as dangerous

8 The cat has got _____ food on its plate than the dog.
   a the least
   b less

3 **Complete the text with the comparative or the superlative form of these adjectives.**

big   delicious   ~~good~~   interesting   near   pretty   quick   scary

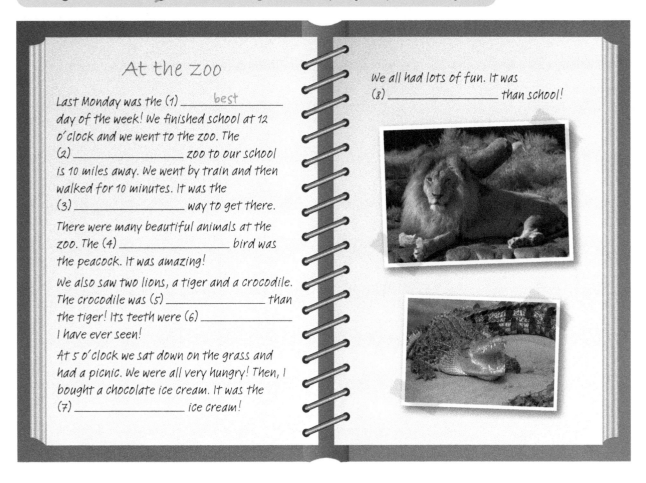

At the zoo

Last Monday was the (1) _____best_____ day of the week! We finished school at 12 o'clock and we went to the zoo. The (2) _____ zoo to our school is 10 miles away. We went by train and then walked for 10 minutes. It was the (3) _____ way to get there.

There were many beautiful animals at the zoo. The (4) _____ bird was the peacock. It was amazing!

We also saw two lions, a tiger and a crocodile. The crocodile was (5) _____ than the tiger! Its teeth were (6) _____ I have ever seen!

At 5 o'clock we sat down on the grass and had a picnic. We were all very hungry! Then, I bought a chocolate ice cream. It was the (7) _____ ice cream!

We all had lots of fun. It was (8) _____ than school!

 **Speaking**

Talk to your partner about your family, friends and school subjects, using the comparative and superlative forms.

My brother is taller than me.

My father is the tallest in our family.

12 Be going to

It's very cold today and tomorrow is going to be a snowy day!

The next day...

Um, Matt, look at the sky. It isn't going to snow.

Be going to

We use **be going to**

- to talk about future plans and intentions.
  I'm going to play in the park this afternoon.
- to predict that something is going to happen, when we have some proof or some information.
  The sky is blue. It's going to be a nice day.

Be going to is followed by the bare infinitive.
We're going to visit our grandparents tonight.

Affirmative	Negative
I'm going to make	I'm not going to make
you're going to make	you aren't going to make
he's going to make	he isn't going to make
she's going to make	she isn't going to make
it's going to make	it isn't going to make
we're going to make	we aren't going to make
you're going to make	you aren't going to make
they're going to make	they aren't going to make

Question	Short answers	
Am I going to make ...?	Yes, I am.	No, I'm not.
Are you going to make ...?	Yes, you are.	No, you aren't.
Is he going to make ...?	Yes, he is.	No, he isn't.
Is she going to make ...?	Yes, she is.	No, she isn't.
Is it going to make ...?	Yes, it is.	No, it isn't.
Are we going to make ...?	Yes, we are.	No, we aren't.
Are you going to make ...?	Yes, you are.	No, you aren't.
Are they going to make ...?	Yes, they are.	No, they aren't.

We form the affirmative with **am, are** or **is, going to** and the bare infinitive.
Karen is going to make a cake for the party.

We form the negative with **am, are** or **is**, the word **not**, **going to** and the bare infinitive.
Andrew and Jason are not going to play football this evening.

We form questions with **am, are** or **is, going to** or the bare infinitive.
Is Bianca going to visit us?

We form short answers with **am, are** or **is**. We don't use **going to** or the main verb.
Are you going to meet Elizabeth?
Yes, I am.
Is Alexander going to go to Australia?
No, he isn't.

Time Expressions

We often use the following time expressions with **be going to**, they go at the beginning or at the end of the sentence: **tonight, tomorrow, soon, later on, in the morning/evening, this afternoon/weekend, next week/year, in a week/month** etc.
This summer we're going to travel to India.
We're going to stay at home this evening.

Remember!

I'm = I am
you're = you are
he's = he is
she's = she is
it's = it is
we're = we are
they're = they are

1 **Complete the sentences with be going to. Use the verb in brackets.**

1   The clouds are very black. It __'s going to rain__ . (rain)

2   This weekend we _____ with our grandparents. (stay)

3   My parents _____ me a laptop for my birthday. (get)

4   I can hear footsteps. They _____ us! (find)

5   It's sunny. You _____ a lovely day at the beach. (have)

6   Phillip _____ Egypt in February. (visit)

7   Be careful! You _____ . (fall)

8   Cathy and I _____ to the cinema tonight. (go)

2 **Complete the sentences with the negative form of be going to. Use the verbs in brackets.**

1   I __'m not going to tidy__ my bedroom tonight. (tidy)

2   My sister _____ to the party. She wasn't invited. (go)

3   This puzzle is very difficult. We _____ it today. (finish)

4   They're terrible singers! They _____ the song contest. (win)

5   Mum _____ me the laptop. It's very expensive. (buy)

6   It's sunny. I _____ my raincoat to school. (wear)

3 **Complete the questions using be going to and the words in brackets. Then complete the short answers.**

1   _____ Is Max going to take _____ an umbrella? (Max / take)
    No, __he isn't__ .

2   _____ your homework tonight? (you / do)
    Yes, _____ .

3   _____ in the cave? (they / sleep)
    No, _____ .

4   _____ to the moon? (the astronaut / travel)
    Yes, _____ .

5   _____ the invitations this afternoon? (you / send)
    No, _____ .

6   _____ the British museum in London? (Vicky / visit)
    Yes, _____ .

4 **Complete the text with be going to. Use the verbs in brackets.**

Every Saturday, Josh and I play basketball but tomorrow we
(1) __aren't going to play__ (not play). Mum and Dad
(2) _____ (take) us to the mountains because
it (3) _____ (snow). I can't wait!
We (4) _____ (wake up) at 6.30 in the morning and
Dad (5) _____ (drive) us to the mountains. I like
travelling by car and I usually fall asleep!
Josh and I (6) _____ (go) skiing. We're not very good
but we like it. Mum and Dad (7) _____ (not try) it.
They want to watch us!
It (8) _____ (be) a very exciting day.

5 Look at the pictures and complete the sentences with **be going to**. Use these verbs.

go   have   make   ~~ride~~   visit   watch

1 On Monday, I ____'m going to ride____ _____ my bike near the river.

2 On Tuesday, Dad and I _____ _____ a kite.

3 On Wednesday, I _____ _____ sailing in the lake with Andy.

4 On Thursday, we _____ _____ a DVD at Jude's house.

5 On Friday, we _____ _____ a picnic on the beach.

6 On Saturday, I _____ _____ my grandparents in the countryside.

 **Speaking**

Talk to your partner about what you are going to do this summer. Use the suggestions to help you.

I'm going to visit my cousins in Sydney.

Wow! I'm going to learn Japanese.

- trips/journeys/holidays
- outdoor activities
- entertainment
- unusual plans

Future Simple

Future Simple

We use the **Future Simple**

- to predict the future.
  People will live on other planets one day.
- for decisions we make at the time of speaking.
  We'll come for a walk, too.
- when we want to offer help.
  I'll come and help you plant some trees.
- for promises, threats and warnings.
  I'll take you for a swim, I promise.
- to ask somebody to do something for us.
  Will you walk to the beach with me, please?
- after phrases such as **I think, I'm sure, I hope, I bet**, etc.
  I'm sure we'll save the rainforest.

We form the affirmative with **will** and the bare infinitive.
Cathy and I will buy the presents.

We form the negative with **will**, the word **not** and the bare infinitive.
Stevie will not help me with my homework.

We form questions with **will** and the bare infinitive.
Will Alex come with us?

We form short answers with **will** or **won't**. We don't use the main verb.
Will you meet Paul tonight?
Yes, I will.
Will it rain tomorrow?
No, it won't.

Affirmative	Negative
I'll come (will come)	I won't come (will not come)
you'll come (will come)	you won't come (will not come)
he'll come (will come)	he won't come (will not come)
she'll come (will come)	she won't come (will not come)
it'll come (will come)	it won't come (will not come)
we'll come (will come)	we won't come (will not come)
you'll come (will come)	you won't come (will not come)
they'll come (will come)	they won't come (will not come)

Question	Short answers	
Will I come ...?	Yes, I will.	No, I won't.
Will you come ...?	Yes, you will.	No, you won't.
Will he come ...?	Yes, he will.	No, he won't.
Will she come ...?	Yes, she will.	No, she won't.
Will it come ...?	Yes, it will.	No, it won't.
Will we come ...?	Yes, we will.	No, we won't.
Will you come ...?	Yes, you will.	No, you won't.
Will they come ...?	Yes, they will.	No, they won't.

Time Expressions
We often use the following time expressions with the **Future Simple**, they go at the beginning or at the end of a sentence:
tonight, tomorrow, soon, later on, in the morning/evening, this afternoon/weekend, next week/year, in a week/month etc.
I'll study this evening.
Tomorrow I'll go mountain climbing with you.

1 Match.

1 It's a lovely morning   a I'm sure you'll have a great time.
2 I'm going to a party tonight.   b Don't worry, I'll help you with it.
3 Let's take Mum skiing for her birthday.   c John and I will walk to school.
4 It's really hot.   d She will enjoy it.
5 Don't cut down any more trees.   e I think I'll have a cold drink.
6 I can't do my science homework!   f You'll destroy the park.

2 Make the sentences negative.

1 Mum and Dad will put up our tent.
   Mum and Dad won't put up our tent.   .

2 Uncle Todd will take us to the amusement park.
   _____ .

3 They'll sleep in the igloo.
   _____ .

4 It'll be foggy tomorrow morning.
   _____ .

5 Isabel will win the race.
   _____ .

6 We'll look for information about the planets.
   _____ .

3 Write questions with the Future Simple. Then complete the short answers.

1 Amy / talk about / rainforests
   Will Amy talk about rainforests?
   Yes, _____ she will _____ .

2 Josh and Kate / bring / photos / of waterfalls
   _____
   No, _____ .

3 Susie and I / talk about / about our holiday
   _____
   No, _____ .

4 Robbie / give / me / book / about wild animals
   _____
   Yes, _____ .

5 Mum / walk / in the forest / with me
   _____
   Yes, _____ .

6 you / show us / pictures of the canyon
   _____
   No, _____ .

4 **Look at the pictures and complete the sentences with the Future Simple. Use these verbs.**

~~carry~~   fly   get   have   buy   swim

This picnic basket is very heavy.

1 I ___'ll carry___ it for you.

Do you want some lemonade?

2 No, I _____ any, thanks.

Bye Mum!

Don't go out, you _____ wet.

3

What a pretty butterfly!

4 Don't shout. It _____ away.

The sea is dirty!

5 You're right. We _____ here.

There isn't any juice Mum.

6 I _____ some from the supermarket.

 **Speaking**

Talk with your partner about what you will do to help protect the environment. Use the suggestions to help you.

I'll use less water when I shower.

That's a good idea. I'll pick up rubbish at the beach.

- clean the streets
- pick up rubbish at the beach
- plant trees
- use less paper / save water
- talk to people about rainforests

Review 6

Units 11 & 12

1 **Complete the sentences with the comparative form of the adjectives in brackets.**

1 My German mark was _____lower_____ than Sarah's. (low)

2 Your carnival costume is _____ than my costume. (good)

3 Chinese is _____ than French. (difficult)

4 Comics are _____ than books. (exciting)

5 The rain is _____ than it was yesterday. (heavy)

6 The bus stop is _____ than the train station. (far)

2 **Complete the sentences with the superlative form of the adjectives in brackets.**

1 Volleyball is ____the most popular____ sport at our school. (popular)

2 That was _____ cycling race! (good)

3 Yesterday was _____ day of the month. (cloudy)

4 Clare's boots are _____ of all. (expensive)

5 *The Nightmare before Christmas* is _____ film. (scary)

6 Nicky is _____ girl in our school. (tall)

3 **Complete the sentences with as ... as and not as ... as and the adjectives in brackets.**

1 Dad is 38 years old. Mum is 34 years old.
   Dad is ____not as young as____ Mum. (young)

2 In England it is often cold. In Greece, it's usually hot.
   England is _____ Greece. (hot)

3 The museum building is 30 metres tall. The cinema building is also 30 metres tall.
   The museum building is _____ the cinema building. (tall)

4 Fifteen students in my class enjoy science lessons. Twenty-five students enjoy history lessons.
   Science lessons are _____ history lessons. (popular)

5 Helen's suitcase weighs 15 kilos. Kendra's suitcase also weighs 15 kilos.
   Kendra's suitcase is _____ Helen's suitcase. (heavy)

6 Tim's mobile phone costs €60. Jack's mobile phone costs €70.
   Jack's mobile phone is _____ Tim's. (cheap)

4 **Complete the sentences with the Future Simple. Use the verbs in brackets.**

1 I _____'ll give_____ you your medicine. (give)

2 I promise we _____ a trick on you. (not play)

3 You can use Dad's laptop. I _____ him. (not tell)

4 There's someone at the front door. _____ it? (you / open)

5 _____ the houseboat? (they / sell)

6 _____ lost? (we / get)

7 Dad _____ you to the airport. (drive)

8 The skiing holiday _____ great! (be)

5 Look at the pictures and complete the questions using **be going to** and the words in brackets. Then write short answers.

1 _____Is Luke going to win_____ the race?
(Luke / win)
_____No, he isn't._____

2 _____ in the library today? (you / study)
_____

3 _____ a bus?
(they / catch)
_____

4 _____ cold today?
(it / be)
_____

PARTY
Dear Fiona
Please come to my birthay on Saturday at 6o'clock. We'll have a great time.
from Nadia

5 _____ a party for her birthday? (Nadia / have)
_____

6 _____ new trees?
(they / plant)
_____

6 Complete the text with the correct form of **be going to**. Use the verbs in brackets.

Next week, Mum, Dad, Tom and I (1) _____are going to go_____ (go) on a walking holiday in the mountains. I often go to the mountains because my cousins live nearby and we all love walking and cycling.

Dad (2) _____ (not drive) because we
(3) _____ (travel) by train. We
(4) _____ (stop) at our grandparents' farm for lunch. Grandma and Grandad have got lots of animals!

This year, we (5) _____ (not sleep) at my cousins' house. We (6) _____ (stay) in a lovely hotel and we (7) _____ (take part) in a long walk with lots of other people. I (8) _____ (not cycle) this time.
We (9) _____ (have) a great time!

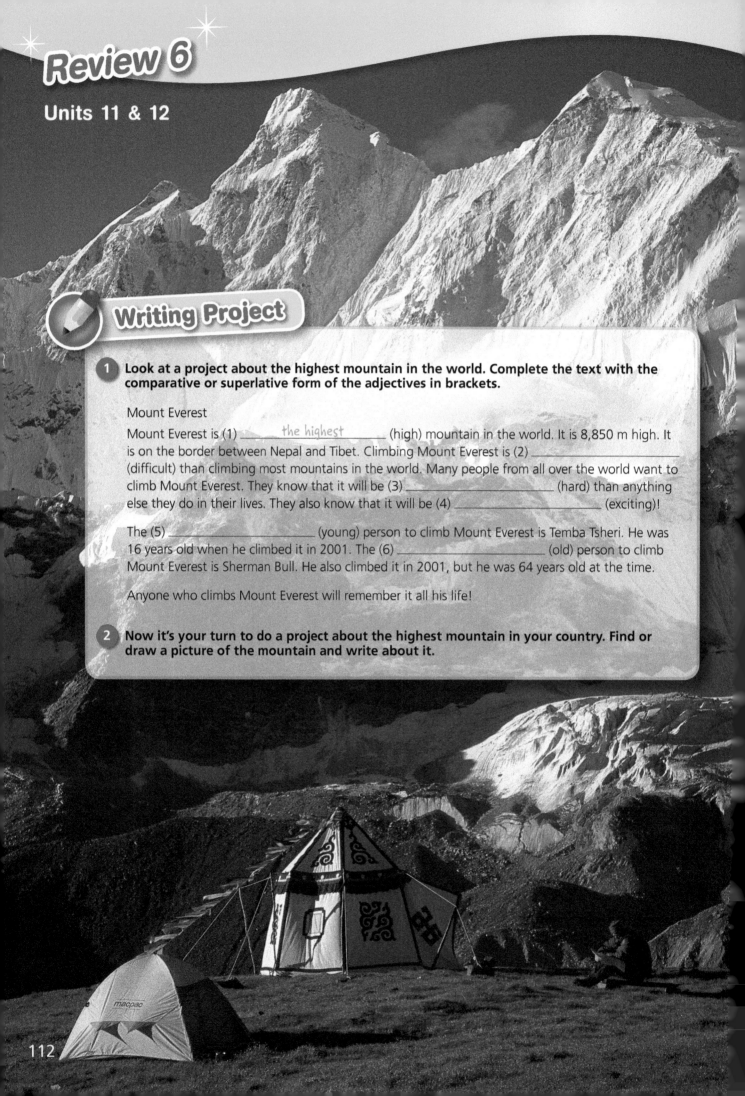

Review 6

Units 11 & 12

Writing Project

1 Look at a project about the highest mountain in the world. Complete the text with the comparative or superlative form of the adjectives in brackets.

Mount Everest

Mount Everest is (1) _____the highest_____ (high) mountain in the world. It is 8,850 m high. It is on the border between Nepal and Tibet. Climbing Mount Everest is (2) _____ (difficult) than climbing most mountains in the world. Many people from all over the world want to climb Mount Everest. They know that it will be (3) _____ (hard) than anything else they do in their lives. They also know that it will be (4) _____ (exciting)!

The (5) _____ (young) person to climb Mount Everest is Temba Tsheri. He was 16 years old when he climbed it in 2001. The (6) _____ (old) person to climb Mount Everest is Sherman Bull. He also climbed it in 2001, but he was 64 years old at the time.

Anyone who climbs Mount Everest will remember it all his life!

2 Now it's your turn to do a project about the highest mountain in your country. Find or draw a picture of the mountain and write about it.

Irregular verbs

Infinitive	Past Simple	Infinitive	Past Simple
be	was/were	lie	lay
become	became	light	lit
break	broke	make	made
bring	brought	meet	met
buy	bought	put	put
build	built	read	read
catch	caught	ride	rode
choose	chose	run	ran
come	came	say	said
cost	cost	see	saw
cut	cut	sell	sold
do	did	send	sent
draw	drew	shine	shone
drink	drank	shoot	shot
drive	drove	sing	sang
eat	ate	sit	sat
fall	fell	sleep	slept
feed	fed	speak	spoke
feel	felt	spend	spent
fly	flew	stand	stood
find	found	steal	stole
forget	forgot	swim	swam
get	got	take	took
give	gave	teach	taught
go	went	tear	tore
have	had	tell	told
hear	heard	think	thought
hide	hid	throw	threw
hold	held	understand	understood
keep	kept	wake	woke
know	knew	wear	wore
lose	lost	win	won
leave	left	write	wrote

Word list

Introduction

album (n)
amazing (adj)
beach (n)
box (n)
dinner (n)
exciting (adj)
foot (n)
funny (adj)
game (n)
giraffe (n)
hospital (n)
hour (n)
hut (n)
island (n)
kitchen (n)
knife (n)
lady (n)
leaf (n)
life (n)
mouse (n)
nice (adj)
pet (n)
phone (n)
photo (n)
roof (n)
ruler (n)
sheep (n)
spider (n)
tooth (n)
toy (n)
warm (adj)
watch (n)
wife (n)
woman (n)

UNIT ONE

Lesson One

chimp (n)

clever (adj)
cool (adj)
crazy about (expr)
hungry (adj)
meet (v)
old (adj)
on holiday (expr)
science (n)
scientist (n)
shark (n)
sky (n)
trick (n)
ugly (adj)
very (adv)
young (adj)

Lesson Two

dark (adj)
doll (n)
fair (adj)
hair (n)
hotel (n)
job (n)
keep (v)
long (adj)
next to (prep)
penguin (n)
rabbit (n)

Lesson Three

arm (n)
chick (n)
daughter (n)
favourite (adj)
hand (n)
husband (n)
near (prep)
twin (n)

UNIT TWO

Lesson One

board game (n)

boot (n)

camera (n)

city (n)

computer game (n)

dragon (n)

fast (adj)

lizard (n)

magic (adj)

map (n)

message (n)

mobile phone (n)

museum (n)

mystery (n)

piece (n)

puzzle (n)

real (adj)

strange (adj)

teddy bear (n)

work (n)

Lesson Two

astronaut (n)

bedroom (n)

chimpanzee (n)

globe (n)

moon (n)

scary (adj)

shop window (n)

the Antarctic (n)

thing (n)

town (n)

REVIEW 1

bottle (n)

centimetre (n)

close to (prep)

coral reef (n)

floor (n)

food (n)

grandparent (n)

grow (v)

kind (n)

live (v)

project (n)

UNIT THREE

Lesson One

art (n)

brush (v)

calculator (n)

carry (v)

clean (v)

come (v)

every (adj)

fix (v)

geography (n)

live (v)

miss (v)

sit (v)

snow (v)

stay (v)

study (v)

subject (n)

teach (v)

tidy (v)

touch (v)

use (v)

wash (v)

Lesson Two

after (prep)

bookcase (n)

breakfast (n)

cafeteria (n)

club (n)

cook (v)

get up (phr v)

helmet (n)

history (n)

Japanese (adj)

karaoke (n)

library (n)

lunch (n)

playground (n)

team (n)

uniform (n)

wear (v)

Lesson Three

buy (v)

diary (n)

finish (v)

love (v)

magazine (n)

only (adv)

scared (adj)

see (v)

sum (n)

test (n)

twice (adv)

UNIT FOUR

Lesson One

Chinese (adj)

coin (n)

collect (v)

collection (n)

competition (n)

drink (n)

interesting (adj)

spell (v)

stamp (n)

start (v)

think (v)

What's the matter? (expr)

Lesson Two

amusement park (n)

catch (v)

difficult (adj)

ferris wheel (n)

find (v)

fly (v)

ice-skating (n)

merry-go-round (n)

money (n)

move (v)

ride (n)

rollercoaster (n)

send (v)

skates (n)

Sorry! (expr)

REVIEW 2

building (n)

centre (n)

famous (adj)

marble (adj)

need (v)

outside (prep)

ring (v)

sad (adj)

sports centre (n)

surprising (adj)

together (adv)

water tank (n)

wonder (n)

UNIT FIVE

Lesson One

boring (adj)

candle (n)

careful (adj)

classmate (n)

costume (n)

cut (v)

face (n)

festival (n)

invite (v)

lake (n)

late (adj)

next (adj)

paint (n)

pop music (n)

put away (phr v)

seat (n)

stall (n)

throw (v)

walk (n)

Lesson Two

carton (n)

count (v)

crisps (n)

cup (n)

delicious (adj)

fireworks (n)

loaf (n)

mean (v)

packet (n)

slice (n)

time (n)

Lesson Three

April Fool's day (n)

Bonfire Night (n)

Christmas (n)

clue (n)

invitation (n)

joke (n)

play (n)

ticket (n)

wait (v)

witch (n)

UNIT SIX

Lesson One

biscuit (n)

cheese (n)

dessert (n)

ice (n)

meal (n)

meat (n)

parade (n)

plate (n)

visitor (n)

waiter (n)

Lesson Two

basket (n)

butter (n)

chicken (n)

chip (n)

crepe (n)

ham (n)

hole (n)

Indian (adj)

juice (n)

mustard (n)

rice (n)

REVIEW 3

before (prep)

coast (n)

cupboard (n)

dolphin (n)

enemy (n)

fancy-dress (adj)

forget (v)

hide (v)

honey (n)

pair (n)

protect (v)

rubbish (n)

serve (v)

sugar (n)

tell a joke (expr)

treasure hunt (n)

unusual (adj)

whale (n)

UNIT SEVEN

Lesson One

at the moment (exp)

chase (v)

cross (v)

cycle (v)

dive (v)

egg and spoon race (n)

enter (v)

fall (v)

finish line (n)

hold (v)

leave (v)

lie (v)

more and more (expr)

practise (v)

prize (n)

push (v)

sail (v)

son (n)

these days (expr)

trainers (n)

travel (v)

win (v)

Lesson Two

box (v)
call me (expr)
champion (n)
enjoy (v)
feel (v)
gymnast (n)
kick (v)
loud (adj)
match (n)
mountain (n)
sweet (n)
train (v)

Lesson Three

championship (n)
I can't wait! (expr)
the Olympic Games (n)
plan (n)
special (adj)
summer camp (n)
take part (v)
village (n)

UNIT EIGHT

Lesson One

castle (n)
cottage (n)
desert (n)
flat (n)
ghost (n)
guard (n)
houseboat (n)
inside (prep)
noise (n)
same (adj)
scare (v)
shine (v)
stairs (n)
the Tower of London (n)
tree house (n)

Lesson Two

dentist (n)
dirty (adj)

early (adj)
expensive (adj)
friendly (adj)
junk food (n)
pilot (n)
quiet (adj)
vegetable (n)
wake up (phr v)

REVIEW 4

adult (n)
athlete (n)
chew (v)
chewing gum (n)
coach (n)
contest (n)
edge (n)
fire (n)
nature (n)
popular (adj)
relax (v)
shout (v)
spend (v)
try (v)
view (n)

UNIT NINE

Lesson One

ago (adv)
camel (n)
cheap (adj)
cloud (n)
countryside (n)
last (adj)
magician (n)
minute (n)
passenger (n)
passport (n)
pyramid (n)
sand (n)
suitcase (n)
swimsuit (n)
tent (n)

terrible (adj)

thirsty (adj)

trip (n)

yesterday (n)

Lesson Two

airport (n)

arrive (v)

bus stop (n)

cry (v)

decide (v)

dry (v)

fit (v)

flight (n)

land (v)

port (n)

ship (n)

the Eiffel Tower (n)

tie (v)

Lesson Three

break (v)

campsite (n)

clothes (pl n)

sell (v)

shell (n)

story (n)

sun cream (n)

take (v)

travel agency (n)

wonderful (adj)

UNIT TEN

Lesson One

actor (n)

audience (n)

autograph (n)

concert (n)

drive (v)

film studio (n)

interview (n)

role (n)

shoot (v)

Lesson Two

acting (n)

adventure film (n)

award (n)

company (n)

horror film (n)

lose (v)

medal (n)

musical (n)

romance (n)

smile (v)

western (n)

REVIEW 5

Ancient Egypt (n)

become (v)

coffin (n)

cruise ship (n)

die (v)

discover (v)

gold (adj)

mummy (n)

purse (n)

tomb (n)

UNIT ELEVEN

Lesson One

binoculars (n)

butterfly (n)

clean (adj)

far (adj)

heavy (adj)

height (n)

high (adj)

horrible (adj)

intelligent (adj)

lazy (adj)

leopard (n)

mark (n)

path (n)

price (n)

serious (adj)

tiny (adj)

torch (n)

weight (n)

wide (adj)

Lesson Two

dinosaur (n)

easy (adj)

goldfish (n)

important (adj)

insect (n)

kind (adj)

neighbourhood (n)

peacock (n)

pony (n)

silly (adj)

slow (adj)

tail (n)

tasty (adj)

tortoise (n)

Lesson Three

bright (adj)

cave (n)

pirate (n)

quick (adj)

street (n)

worm (n)

UNIT TWELVE

Lesson One

activity (n)

entertainment (n)

footsteps (n)

journey (n)

lovely (adj)

outdoor (adj)

raincoat (n)

snowy (adj)

Lesson Two

canyon (n)

cut down (phr v)

destroy (v)

foggy (adj)

forest (n)

information (n)

paper (n)

pick up (phr v)

planet (n)

plant (v)

promise (v)

put up (v)

rainforest (n)

save (v)

waterfall (n)

wild (adj)

REVIEW 6

anything else (expr)

border (n)

cost (v)

get lost (expr)

hard (adj)

low (adj)

nearby (prep)

weigh (v)